Multiplying Leaders in Intercultural Contexts

Endorsements

There is no shortage of books on leadership these days, but there are not many on the related intercultural issues, and those publications rarely achieve what this book does. Evelyn and Richard start from an acknowledgement that leadership is not something we export or install; leadership is part of human life and every culture has forms and levels of leadership. This practical book explores how to identify and develop leaders within their cultural context. Because we all have our own cultural lenses, it is easy for foreign workers to look for what most aligns with their own expectations when identifying leaders and to facilitate training accordingly. This book is packed with real life examples and helps us to re-examine our expectations and understanding of what leadership is, how we can best nurture it, and, of course, how to best apply biblical principles.

Often when we hear the word "leadership," our first thought is of senior leaders, heads of substantial bodies and networks, etc., but leadership happens at every level and developing leadership in appropriate ways from the lowest levels up works for greater healthiness overall and this should not be neglected. This book approaches the subject from a radically different angle than many others.

This is a great follow up to their book on intercultural disciple making and integrating as it does awareness of cultural dynamics with the practicalities of leadership development. I would hope that many working around the world will patiently and repeatedly work through this material as they learn to serve fruitfully in various contexts.

Colin Bearup
Cross-cultural worker and trainer for over 35 years
Visiting Lecturer, Sydney Missionary & Bible College and the Nazarene
Theological College in the UK; Author, *Clues to Africa, Islam, and the Gospel*

Perhaps the most difficult and most important step in cross-cultural church planting is leadership development. I once heard a pastor from the Middle East say to a group of missionaries, "We need missionaries who want to work themselves out of a job ASAP! Let the nationals be the pastors." *Multiplying Leaders in Intercultural Contexts* provides church planters with a practical guide for this important aspect of church planting. The emphases on the influence of culture on leadership and developing leaders at all levels of ministry are important contributions of *Multiplying Leaders in Intercultural Contexts* that are often overlooked in books on leadership development. Evelyn and Richard write from years of experience in cross-cultural ministry and have provided the missionary community a valuable church-planting resource.

Ed Grudier
Director of the Centre for Cross-Cultural Mission,
Sydney Missionary and Bible College

Evelyn and Richard Hibbert have provided practical insights into the journey of leadership development in intercultural situations. This book is a guide to intentional practices that recognise the diversity that is the body of Christ. It calls all those involved in developing leaders to consider context, create space, learn to listen, and continue their own discipleship journey as part of new communities of Jesus followers. I found myself reflecting on many of my own experiences, engaging the practical principles of this book that are set out so clearly. All those engaged in intercultural contexts should add this book to their reading list as it calls us to live the everyday faith journey in discipling, being discipled and growing community.

CATHY HINE
Co-Founder and Coordinator, When Women Speak
Mentor, Angelina Noble Centre; Director, Interserve International

The key to reaching the nations with the gospel is to see movements of reproducing churches, and the key to healthy church planting movements is the development of adequate numbers of leaders. Evelyn and Richard Hibbert's latest book is packed with academic reflections and practical insights based on their experience of training leaders in the Millet revival in Bulgaria, and years of teaching students in Australia. The book is written for cross-cultural "leadership developers," recognising that the missionary's primary task is not to be the heroic, lone ranger church planter, but to nurture and facilitate the development of national leaders.

Richard Hibbert passed away in November 2020, and this book is part of his legacy, embodying his commitment to mission and leadership. I warmly recommend this book to anyone who shares his concern to see godly leaders equipped and able to shepherd growing churches among unreached peoples.

JULYAN LIDSTONE
Ambassador, Muslim Ministries of OM International

Evelyn and Richard call us to an incarnational style of leadership development that goes beyond simple method. This book challenges cross-cultural workers to understand leadership formation in the host culture and adapt training appropriately. We especially liked the 4Cs (Community, Character, Clarity, Care) and the four chapters where they were fleshed out. *Multiplying Leaders in Intercultural Contexts* is a must read for any cross-cultural trainer who desires to equip local leadership. Don't formulate your strategic plan until you have read this book!

CAROLYN AND JERRY MOYER
(Carolyn) Executive Director, World Team Australia
(Jerry) Director, World Team Europe

So much experience, thought, and Bible-tempered practical wisdom has been poured into this book to make it a treasure chest of help for rookie (and veteran) cross-cultural workers—especially church planters and disciplers hoping to raise up leaders fit for the task of leading Jesus's church wherever it might be. The book has us wishing it had been written a lot earlier—like thirty years ago! It cracks one's mind out of inadvertent cultural routines. The strength of the book—and its thesis—is that it insists that a leader is every bit a disciple as the disciples he or she is to lead. This means training leaders in their natural context; their community. So, the theory makes sense. But the beauty of the book is that it makes practical sense of the theory all the way to the final chapters when the practical is delivered almost blow-by-blow. With so much to absorb we can see the book becoming the *Where There Is No Doctor* for the cross-cultural leader-developing Christian worker.

ROSS AND LYNDAL WEBB
Bible translators for over 30 years, Wycliffe Australia

Multiplying Leaders in Intercultural Contexts

Recognizing and Developing Grassroots Potential

Evelyn and Richard Hibbert

Multiplying Leaders in Intercultural Contexts: Recognizing and Developing Grassroots Potential

© 2023 by Evelyn and Richard Hibbert. All rights reserved.

No part of this book may be reproduced, stored in a retrieval system, or transmitted in any form or by any means—electronic, mechanical, photocopy, recording, or otherwise—without prior written permission from the publisher, except brief quotations used in connection with reviews in magazines or newspapers. For permission, email permissions@wclbooks.com. For corrections, email editor@wclbooks.com.

Scripture quotations are taken from the Holy Bible, New Living Translation, copyright © 1996, 2004, 2015 by Tyndale House Foundation. Used by permission of Tyndale House Publishers, Inc., Carol Stream, Illinois 60188. All rights reserved.

Published by William Carey Publishing
10 W. Dry Creek Cir
Littleton, CO 80120 | www.missionbooks.org

William Carey Publishing is a ministry of Frontier Ventures
Pasadena, CA | www.frontierventures.org

Cover and Interior Designer: Mike Riester

ISBNs: 978-1-64508-445-7 (paperback)
978-1-64508-447-1 (epub)

Printed Worldwide

27 26 25 24 23   1 2 3 4 5   IN

Library of Congress Control Number: 2022950292

This book is dedicated to the memory of my husband, Richard.

*Richard's concern for leaders across the world
meant that he worked on this book right up until two days before
he went to join his beloved Lord, in November 2020.*

*May the fruit of his labor be many leaders empowered to lead churches
that multiply, throughout all cultures, to the ends of the earth.*

Contents

Preface	xi
Chapter 1: Grow the Edge of the Church	**1**
Focus on Groups	2
Reproduce Life	4
Find the Followers and the People Who Pass Things On	7
Develop People, Not Programs	8
Examine Ourselves	9
Book Outline	11
Chapter 2: Value Cultural Difference	**13**
Understand How Culture Affects Leadership	13
Adjust Our Approach according to Culture	18
Chapter 3: Investigate Leadership Dimensions of Culture	**21**
Gauge Power Distance	23
Research Paternalistic Expectations	25
Determine Tolerance for Uncertainty	28
Pay Attention to Context	30
Look at Groups	33
Explore Group Influence on Individuals	36
Learn with Humility	37
Chapter 4: Disciple Leaders Like All Other Disciples	**41**
Test Leaders First as Disciples	43
Identify Exemplary Disciples	44
Foster Continuing Growth	45
Remember That We Are Also Disciples	46
Chapter 5: Identify All the Leaders	**49**
Identify the Growing-Edge Leaders	50
Focus on the Majority	55
Chapter 6: Foster Biblical Leadership	**57**
Strengthen the 4 Cs—Community, Character, Clarity, Care	57
Apply Biblical Metaphors Carefully	58
Nurture Life in All Its Fullness	60
Promote One-Another Care	62
Cultivate Generosity	63

Chapter 7: Guard against Leaders' Vulnerabilities — 67
Research Vulnerabilities and Accountability — 72
Model Self-Awareness — 73

Chapter 8: Strengthen the Community (C1) — 75
Keep Leaders in Their Communities — 76
Look for Community Endorsement — 80
Strengthen Community Decision-Making Processes — 82
Include the Community in Leaders' Development — 83
Promote Community Values through Group-Based Learning — 85

Chapter 9: Build Character (C2) — 87
Strengthen Capacity for Pain-Bearing — 88
Model Integrity and Transparency — 91
Support God's Forging of Christian Character — 93
Be Examples — 95

Chapter 10: Clarify the Community's Purpose (C3) — 99
Promote Clear Vision — 99
Help Leaders Craft Collective Vision — 103
Encourage Clear Communication — 108
Encourage Vision Review — 109

Chapter 11: Develop Care across the Community (C4) — 113
Lift Up Carers — 114
Nurture Healthy Relationships — 115
Share Life Together — 118
Coordinate Believers' Gifts — 120
Build the Local Community — 121

Chapter 12: What Should We, as Developers, Do? — 125
Build Relationships — 125
Be Models — 126
Research the Culture — 128
Contextualize — 131
Adjust Our Methods and Expectations — 132
Mediate — 134
Become Reflective Practitioners — 136

Chapter 13: Leadership-Development Principles	**137**
1. Disciple Leaders Like All Other Disciples	138
2. Select Leaders Who Are Endorsed by Their Communities	139
3. Include the Community around the Leader and Strengthen It	140
4. Develop the 4 Cs	142
5. Connect Knowledge with Experience	148
Chapter 14: Putting Leadership-Development into Practice	**153**
Context 1—Pioneer Church Planting	153
Context 2—Movement of Multiplying Churches	154
Context 3—Churches in Contexts Where Pastors Are Expected to Attend Bible Colleges	157
Do Life with Leaders	159
Acknowledgments	161
About the Authors	161
Bibliography	162

Figures

Figure 1: A model for understanding culture (adapted from Hiebert, 2008, 32–33)	14
Figure 2: Variation between and within cultures in scheduling (Organized vs. Flexible)	22
Figure 3: Leadership types and estimated number of each type in a church movement of 10,000 people	54
Figure 4: The four critical characteristics of Christian leadership (4 Cs)	57
Figure 5: The 4 Cs of Christian leadership	58
Figure 6: Photos of shepherds in different parts of the world (USA photo from: https://www.pxfuel.com/en/free-photo-jyeqt, July 8, 2021; Australia photo from: Andrew Phillips, ABC Local News, https://www.abc.net.au/news/2016-07-15/a-farmer-uses-a-quad-bike-to-muster-sheep-across-a/7634004?nw=0, Jul 15, 2016.)	59
Figure 7: Vision in linear time	105
Figure 8: Vision in cyclical time	106
Figure 9: Vision focused on the past	107
Figure 10: Making connections between life and theory	148

Preface

In his work at Sydney Missionary and Bible College (Australia), Richard interacted with many missionaries from around the globe. A constant concern these missionaries expressed was the need for a resource to help them develop grassroots leaders. These leaders usually have had no formal theological training, and sometimes little education. They are often illiterate. However, they are well respected within their communities and are followed by others. Providing this resource was Richard's priority in the final two years of his life.

Richard was a modern-day Barnabas (cf. Acts 4:36). He had a remarkable ability to come alongside people regardless of where they lived, what their background was, whether they were illiterate or had a PhD, and make them feel valued and encouraged. Richard encouraged them, built them up, and empowered them to be the best they could be for God. In this book we urge you too to come alongside existing leaders, to respect and encourage them, as well as learn from them.

The challenge of developing leaders is particularly acute where the church is multiplying rapidly. But even in places where leadership-training programs have existed for a long time, there is often a shortage of trained leaders. After nearly fifty years of theological education being available to the Highland Quichua churches in Ecuador, for example, there is a ten to one ratio of churches to pastors.[1]

Similarly, in India it has been reported that there is only one trained pastor for every six congregations.[2] Indian Christian workers serving in regions where churches are multiplying rapidly are often sent out with very little specific preparation for their ministry context. An in-depth study of growing churches in India revealed that many were led by new believers. A large proportion of these leaders could not read.[3] Church leaders across Asia, Africa, and Latin America say that their number one need is to develop more leaders, as it is estimated that more than two million of their pastors have no training at all.[4]

Most leaders, especially in the Majority World, cannot access leadership development. This is because they are working adults with families. Many leadership-development programs assume that participants will be able to spend time away from their families, jobs, and churches for

---

1 Hunter, "Discipleship Training," 41.
2 Mandryk, *Operation World*, 412.
3 David, "India Leadership Study."
4 Livermore, *Serving with Eyes Wide Open*, 41; cf. Ortiz, "Lessons from TEE," 394.

extended periods. A North American pastor describes his visit to a network of over two hundred churches in northeast Honduras in which most of the pastors are bi-vocational. He writes this about one pastor:

> Perhaps my most poignant memory is of the pastor of the church in Yoro holding the microphone as he prayed in preparation to introduce Bob as the evening's speaker. Gerardo owns an auto repair shop and had come to the church service directly from his shop and would likely return to repairing cars after the service. As I looked at his calloused, unwashed and grease-streaked hands, I thought, "these are the hands of a church planter."[5]

Bi-vocational leaders need to continue in their normal employment to support themselves and their families. They are therefore unable to attend a long-term residential training program. These leaders need to be able to learn and grow without leaving their home churches.

Many leaders feel they cannot train others. They cannot see how to make time for it among all the other demands of ministry. A godly, humble Millet[6] pastor we spoke to recently told us, "I simply don't have the time or resources to give to it." For others, the issue is that they simply do not know how to train leaders. Some don't train others because they don't want to share their power with others. One leader from Ethiopia admitted:

> Let me explain to you what happens when we older leaders see a younger leader with lots of potential coming up. Do you know what we do? … We smash them! … We are afraid the younger leader will come up and take our job, so we make sure that he's stopped before he even gets started![7]

Starting with disciples immersed in a community, Jesus began a movement of multiplying churches, which continues today. Jesus's movement values ordinary people. Each leader, regardless of background, and each community, regardless of size, has a compulsion to share new life with everyone they meet. It is messy, out-of-control, unpredictable, but vibrant and ever-expanding. This is the DNA which Richard and I have sought to nurture and pass on.

---

5 Fields, "Hundreds of Churches in Honduras."
6 The Millet are a Muslim-background, Turkish-speaking people group we have had the privilege of working with in Bulgaria and other parts of Europe.
7 Overstreet, *Unleader*, 33.

CHAPTER

1

GROW THE EDGE OF THE CHURCH

Countless leaders gather people into groups for Jesus's sake across the world. They meet in homes, workplaces, parks, fields, churches, halls, wherever convenient for followers. Leaders share their lives with their followers. Along with their followers, they grow in Christ and introduce him to others. These leaders and their followers are the growing edge of the church. They are learning about and living for Jesus amid normal life.

The leaders we focus on in this book are ordinary people with a passion for Jesus. They are grassroots leaders, settled in their families and communities. They are leaders because they naturally gather people around them. This might be in very small or large groups. They may not be formally appointed (e.g., a woman who starts a group in her home), but sometimes they are (e.g., a cell-group leader).

As long as these groups continue, these leaders faithfully share Jesus with group members. In rapidly growing movements, these leaders catalyze new groups forming. They multiply leaders who start more new groups.

Leaders cannot be separated from their groups. They are firmly embedded in the community of Jesus's disciples. With their followers, leaders clarify the group's specific purpose and bring that purpose into being. They foster the "one-another-ness" that shows the world that they are, together, Christ's disciples. Separating leaders from their communities breaks this mutual bond and makes them vulnerable.

How leaders lead their groups is affected by culture. Likewise, the way groups work is affected by culture. Culture influences the way we communicate and the way we physically arrange ourselves. It controls how much power followers give to leaders and what they expect of them. When we develop leaders across cultures, culture also affects what people expect of us. To multiply disciples and their leaders, what we develop needs to fit in the culture. Christians and non-Christians need to feel that Jesus belongs among them.

The leaders at the growing edge of the church are unlikely to attend Bible college. Many cannot read. They are unable to stop work or leave their families for study. Even if they do go to college, what they study will probably not help them in their day-to-day leadership. Developing these leaders requires a different approach.

We have to find ways of developing them where they are and which help them to apply the Bible practically to what they face in daily life. This book explores the specific needs of these leaders and what we can do to develop them while they remain at home.

If we want to develop leaders, we need to be with them in their communities. As we share in everyday life with them, we become examples in all our human weakness. Our lives are on display. We implant a DNA that will reproduce itself. But we also learn from the community and its leaders.

Whatever we produce, we will gain much more than we give. As you read this book, keep your mind's eye firmly on the people. Developers are people who come alongside leaders, who are people surrounded by people. We mutually learn and grow together.

Focus on Groups

We are communal beings. We need each other. We grow up in families and gather into groups of many types and sizes. One group that Christians gather into is the church. Where his disciples gather, Jesus is there with them (Matt 18:20). Christian leaders are embedded in these communities of Jesus's disciples. But so often when we discuss Christian leaders, we forget the community and focus only on the leader. Without a community of people to lead—without followers—there are no leaders.

> KEEP LEADERS WITH THEIR GROUPS. COME ALONGSIDE LEADERS AND LEARN WITH THEM.

We need to expand our focus beyond the individual leader. Individualistic thinking extracts leaders from their groups. It tends to ignore the interaction between any group and its leaders. A discipline all developers need to cultivate is widening our gaze. We should always include followers whenever we consider leaders.

In contrast to an emphasis on groups, most Christian leadership teaching is strongly biased toward a single, superhero-like, male. This can be an implicit bias. Even if nothing is said, it is the picture in most people's minds. Unfortunately, this bias tends to ignore the many people leading within churches. These leaders may be running Sunday school classes or Bible study groups in established churches. They may be simply gathering people to share the gospel with or teach the Bible to. They may do social justice activities, such as helping widows. They frequently have no official recognition. We wrote this book to facilitate the development of these many, often unrecognized, leaders.

All people in the world belong to ethnolinguistic cultural groups. Some people may belong to more than one ethnolinguistic cultural group. Each person's primary cultural identity incorporates the language learned since early childhood. Along with language, our parents and community teach us cultural values and ways of doing things. Our home language and the culture of our parents is critical to our sense of identity. It is part of how we define who we are in this world. We learn how we fit into our group, who the leaders are, how they should lead, and what we should do in response to their leadership.

Culture, in the ethnolinguistic sense, is often a contested term in today's world. This is usually a reaction against stereotyping. Stereotypes are based on fixed descriptions of cultural traits. They fail to acknowledge the broad range of individuals within cultures. They also do not take into account the constant changes that occur in cultures over time. Yet, no matter how much some people may deny the reality of culture, it still exists. Failure to recognize cultural difference when developing leaders results in ineffective training. It also tends to force leaders to become like leaders in the developers' cultures.

Culture refers to how people perceive their world and act within it. It helps them create and preserve their identity in relation to others. The best way to learn another language and culture is to be fully immersed in it. Without this experience, it is difficult to appreciate how much culture affects who we are and what we do. This includes how we relate to other people. To be effective developers of leaders from other cultures, we need to invest time and effort learning their culture. If there are many cultures where we reside, we will need to learn about all of them. This includes how the different groups interact with each other.

Culture is just one of many groups that people belong to. A local church is another. Together, all the groups in a specific geographical region form a *society*. Societies are larger groups of people, often encompassing many ethnolinguistic cultural groups. We use the term *society* to refer to the broader context in which people live and interact.

There are usually multiple types of groups in any society. Examples of different groups include family, sport, work, professional, and activist groups. Each of these groups defines itself by having rules of belonging. The rules define who belongs. They exclude others. For example, members of a soccer club might have to play soccer and support soccer players.

Whether a group is small or large, its rules determine how the group does things. They outline what to do when conflict arises and the basis for discipline of its members. Leaders are an example for members and others of what it means to belong to the group. They are also usually responsible for enforcing the conditions of belonging.

Societies create rules that enable all their members to live safely together. This is always a negotiated process. It is continually changing as the interests of different groups within a society conflict. Leaders act at the boundaries between different societal groups. Churches are just one set of groups within a society. Christian leaders are accountable to society for what happens within their groups. Paul stresses this in Romans 13:1–7. We have seen this demonstrated in recent years with Western[1] societies holding churches to account for sexual abuse.

Christian leaders do not operate in a vacuum. They are accountable to the groups they lead and the church as a whole, as well as to wider societal standards. It is a good exercise to draw up a map of the different groups that leaders are part of or are affected by. Map the interrelationships between groups. Also map how relationships change as leaders gain responsibility. This helps us understand what the most influential relationships are for each leader. Doing this reinforces for us the embeddedness of leaders in their groups and society. It also makes us aware of the constraints on them and who they are accountable to.

Reproduce Life

Jesus told his followers that he had come so that they could have life in all its fullness. Life reproduces itself. Jesus commanded his disciples to go

---

[1] *The West*, or *Western*, are poorly defined shorthand terms which encompass values that are particularly characteristic of the main missionary-sending, Christian-heritage countries of the last two centuries. These countries have successfully exported their views of theology and leadership around the world. *The West* and *Western* refer to cultural emphases of individualism, rationalism which separates thinking from emotions and embodied experience, and other cultural characteristics that are particularly associated with English- and German-speaking European-background cultures.

As the West has also become associated with higher education, scientific advance, and material prosperity, aspects of Western-ness can be found throughout the world. We use these terms to refer to this complex of values, and leave it to readers to determine how much it applies to themselves or the people they are working with.

and make disciples and pass on everything they had received from him. Jesus did not control his disciples. He left them free to make mistakes, to fail, to have exhilarating success, and to be fully human in all its weakness. Compelled by Jesus's love and example, leaders who follow Jesus reproduce life in all its dynamic out-of-control-ness.

The church is a living community. Life is messy, unpredictable, uncontrollable, and changing all the time. Even when things are settled, a chance event can change everything in an instant. Leaders of small groups and new churches are on the front line in managing life's uncertainty. They work out how biblical faith is relevant to the unpredictability of people's lives. These leaders live out their faith in full view of their followers in the nitty-gritty of real life. They influence others to follow Jesus like they do.

When the good news of Jesus is introduced into new places, it beds down in small groups around local leaders, very often in homes. In this book, we focus on the Lydias, Corneliuses, and Priscillas and Aquilas. They are the non-ordained, often unrecognized, women and men who share their faith and seed new churches wherever they find themselves. Like the home groups of Acts 2:42–47, these mini churches are the building blocks of the larger church in any city or region.

We affirm the many faithful women small group leaders, as well as the working men, who gather people around them in their workplaces, homes, and the places they travel to in their free time. We find these leaders at the living, multiplying edge of the church rather than at its institutional center. As developers, we can learn much from these leaders. We should honor them in our interactions with them and with others.

When we think of leaders, we often think of men at the head of institutions. These institutions are usually associated with big buildings. Institutions and buildings are static, not living, entities. They are built to last a long time. Many people have invested much, emotionally and materially, over a long time, to establish them. With time, the focus of the institution shifts to sustaining itself rather than pursuing its original purpose.

Institutions generate rigid structures to support themselves. These structures include administrative systems, committees, welfare systems, and connections with other institutions. The longer the institution has been around, the more people who join are attracted to its longevity and stability. These people resist change long after the institution has lost its founding purpose or has failed.

Across the West there are many empty church buildings. The last people in them were unable to adapt to the changing world outside the buildings.

The leaders were unable to reproduce life. Our challenge as developers is to help leaders build structures that nurture life rather than suppress it.

Churches usually interface with surrounding society through small groups. Leaders of these groups encourage and equip group members to make new disciples. They help them gather into more small groups. These leaders are embedded in their communities. They manage homes and families, and work in normal jobs.

In contrast, institutional leaders have limited time to engage with the surrounding communities. These leaders focus on maintaining the institution of the church and caring for those who are already Christians. If we, as developers, focus on the institutional center, we will no doubt strengthen the institution. The cost, though, will be paid at its growing edge.

We ask you to lift your eyes off the institutional center. There are many books focused on developing institutional leaders. The institution of the church, not surprisingly, trains its leaders in institutions (Bible colleges and seminaries). There are many books that endlessly discuss the inadequacies of this approach. Some of these books outline ways to tweak the existing programs. We will not extend this echo chamber.

> FOCUS ON THE GROWING EDGE OF THE CHURCH.

If you are preparing for or already teaching in a Bible college with students from other cultures, we recommend studying Craig Ott's *Teaching and Learning Across Cultures*[2] and the book written by multiple authors, *Teaching Across Cultures: A Global Christian Perspective.*[3] If you would like to modify an existing Bible college program, we recommend Perry Shaw's *Transforming Theological Education.*[4] To learn about programs that can be studied by people while they stay in their churches, we recommend learning about Theological Education by Extension (TEE). A good book to help you with this has been produced by the Increase Association.[5] If you would like specific, practical help on how to design learning programs from scratch, we recommend the three books by Robert Ferris, Robert Brynjolfson and Jonathan Lewis, and Jane Vella.[6]

We focus on the growing edge of the church. We explore how we can help the many faithful leaders who labor day after day to grow new disciples.

---

2 Ott, *Teaching and Learning across Cultures*.
3 Shaw et al., eds., *Teaching across Cultures*.
4 Shaw, *Transforming Theological Education*.
5 Burke, Brown, and Qaiser, eds., *TEE for the 21st Century*.
6 Ferris, ed., *Establishing Ministry Training*; Robert Brynjolfson and Jonathan Lewis, eds., *Integral Ministry Training*; Jane Kathryn Vella, *Learning to Listen, Learning to Teach*.

The majority of these leaders will be women,[7] as well as men from ethnolinguistic and socio-economic backgrounds that are not well-represented at the center of the institution. If we only look at the center, these leaders become invisible. Thus, they are often neglected in leadership development.

Find the Followers and the People Who Pass Things On

Small group leaders often emerge naturally. Exercising their Spirit-given gift of leadership with enthusiasm, they spontaneously gather people around themselves. If we encourage and empower them in their ministry, they will naturally reproduce themselves. That is what healthy leaders and churches do. They will often do this in unexpected ways. Then our challenge as developers is not to react negatively to the unexpected. Our aim is to encourage life, not suppress it.

Christian leaders are examples to others of what it means to be disciples of Jesus. Followers recognize that God has gifted leaders to help the group be the people God wants them to be. To be an example does not mean to be perfect. It simply means to be someone who loves Jesus and is growing in relationship with him. However little or much leaders have received, they pass it on to others (Matt 10:8; 2 Tim 2:2). Believers who start new small groups are just as much Christian leaders as pastors of well-established, large congregations.

The best way to start developing leaders is to look for those who are already leading. If they are already leading, their leadership has been acknowledged by their followers. They are likely to have already contextualized Christian leadership for their context. *Contextualization* is the term used for the process through which Christianity comes to belong in a particular cultural setting. This is instead of it being seen as something foreign.

> LOOK FOR THOSE WHO ARE ALREADY LEADING.

If we develop people without experience, they will not have followers' endorsement of their leadership. They will not have tested what it means to be a Christian leader in their context. This means they will be more likely to rely on outsiders to define what Christian leadership looks like. This tends to result in us developing leaders in a way that fits our own cultural background rather than theirs.

---

7 Dana Robert estimates that 80 percent of the world's church are women. "World Christianity as a Women's Movement." See also "Women in World Christianity," https://www.gordonconwell.edu/center-for-global-christianity/research/women-in-world-christianity/.

We are deliberately keeping the definition of Christian leadership simple. We want to include all types of Christian leadership. Our particular focus is on grassroots leaders. These leaders are at the interface between the church and the surrounding world. We especially want to affirm leaders in church-planting situations and the many, many leaders in churches who are not employed as pastors.

Leadership is proven by having followers. Wherever people gather others together for a purpose, they are leading that group. If people say they are leaders but do not have any followers, then they are not leaders. To find the leaders, first look for groups. By observing those groups, we are more likely to learn culturally fitting ways of leading in each specific context.

Christian leadership development is the intentional process of helping leaders, together with their community, become more like Jesus, clarify and implement God-given vision, and strengthen the way community members care for each other. In this book, we focus on developing leaders where the leaders are from a different culture than the developers.

All Christians are growing in Christ throughout their lives. For us, leader development is a lifelong process. It is dynamic, with an ethos of continually passing on what we receive. It can be as simple as a verse at a time, a skill at a time, a response to a life challenge as it arises, all of which can be engaged with, lingered over, and passed on to others easily. We focus as much on passing on as a principle as we focus on the content of what is passed on. Knowledge becomes something that is lived rather than simply a cognitive repository.

Develop People, Not Programs

We refer to the people who are developing leaders as "developers." This emphasizes the broadness of the experience of growing, helping, and supporting leaders. This is in contrast to thinking of developing leaders as just a teaching or training task defined by a training program. We are trying to interrupt the automatic tendency to create programs similar to what happens in schools and colleges. Leadership development is more than a program of study. This is the case even if that program allows leaders to stay in their churches while studying.

Most of the leaders in the world's churches do not have degrees. They will continue to lead effectively without formal theological education. Some leaders will seek out theological education. This may be because they want to learn or because it offers benefits, such as increased status.

Many will be required to get a degree if they want to become an ordained pastor. Many, even if they do seek out a degree, will find that it is not available for their level of school education. They may not be able to study in their own language.

For many, theological education is not accessible geographically or financially. Even if they do manage to do some theological study, it will often not help them to be a better leader. It will rarely give them the skills they need to manage relationships in their groups. It is unlikely to help them engage with the wider community around those groups. Developers, therefore, need to have a different orientation than simply being theological teachers.

To develop these leaders, it is best to begin where they are in terms of their educational experience. Respect the leadership they are already doing. Develop them holistically as people. Foster healthy relationships between people in their groups and with the surrounding community. Learn together with them about how to lead growing churches in their context.

> RESPECT WHAT LEADERS ARE ALREADY DOING.

Examine Ourselves

It is good to stop and reflect on why we want to develop leaders. The prospect of developing leaders raises a lot of questions. For example,

- Who are we thinking of developing?
- Why do we want to develop them?
- What are we intending to develop them to become or to do?
- Do they actually need anything that we have to offer?
- Why do we think *we* should develop them?

Often, the people we are planning to develop will already be more effective in ministry than us. This is not to say that we don't have anything to offer. But often what we do have to offer is less than we think. These reflective questions help to halt the automatic assumption that we are better than those we seek to develop.

One hazard for all teachers, trainers, and developers is a "deficit mentality." If leaders struggle to achieve what we want them to, it is easy to ascribe this to a fault, or deficit, within them. This devalues leaders because they become "a problem" needing to be fixed, rather than people. It positions them as substandard, somehow less than normal. Commonly this occurs because we fail to appreciate how much our own skills have been developed through our own education and personal backgrounds.

For example, many of Evelyn's students in a university in a disadvantaged area of Sydney had never read a whole book before coming to university. Even by the end of their degree programs, they did not appreciate the value of reading books. They also struggled with reading academic papers.

It was easy for lecturers to attribute this to laziness or an unwillingness to learn. However, this attribution failed to appreciate the students' lack of exposure to books in their childhood and schooling.[8] By assuming that the students were lazy, lecturers and the university felt no obligation to invest the time, expense, and effort necessary to help them develop the skills they needed.

When we have a deficit mentality, we forget that the purpose of education is to facilitate learning. Unfortunately, people who are viewed as having deficits, even if they are already leading, are unlikely to be selected for leadership development. A simple example of this is an illiterate leader who is assumed to be unable to do critical thinking, solely on the basis of being unable to read. We have to be careful of our own tendency to assume that because we can read, or have degrees, we are innately better at thinking than others.

Focusing on deficits means that our attention is on fixing the deficits rather than valuing what people bring to the learning experience. This is one of the reasons why we will keep emphasizing that the people we are developing are already leaders. So often in leadership development, developers start by judging the existing leaders. This judgment can relate to leaders' educational level (e.g., illiteracy), assumed moral inadequacies (e.g., intercultural misunderstandings related to lying), or developers' judgments about biblical exegesis inadequacies (e.g., where the Bible is interpreted and applied in ways that are inconsistent with current trends in Western approaches).

The development process then becomes like a crusade to correct the assumed deficiencies. Jesus's response to the tendency that we all have to focus on others' deficiencies is "Do to others whatever you would like them to do to you" (Matt 7:12a). Let's cultivate the discipline of reflecting on our attitudes. Let's aim to root out any tendency toward deficit thinking.

Another reason why we might want to do leadership development is in reaction against our own experience. Sometimes, if our experience has been bad, we react against it. We try to produce the opposite without reflecting on whether the opposite is a good model. Before we start, it is good to reflect on why we think the things that we want to influence for are so important.

---

8 cf. Heath, *Ways with Words*.

A final reflection point for us is to consider whether the method we are planning to use to develop leaders empowers the existing leaders. Sadly, the ways we do leadership development often inadvertently devalue the majority of existing leaders. For example, Selime,[9] a new Muslim-background believer, was passionate in her love for Jesus. She gathered women in house churches. She led her friends and acquaintances to meet Jesus and grow in faith in him.

A Christian leader, John, from an institutional church (not Muslim background), visited Selime. He informed her she should not share her faith, let alone lead groups, unless she first went to Bible college. It was not financially possible for her to attend Bible college. She would also have had to abandon her groups until she was "qualified" to lead them.

John's approach devalued Selime's ministry. His intent was to mold Selime into a pattern of ministry that would have stopped these groups from continuing. There was no other ministry to the women Selime was engaging with. So these women would also have been denied the opportunity of learning about Jesus.

John's visit bewildered and crushed Selime. How much better it would have been if John had encouraged Selime in her leadership. He could have arranged for a culturally sensitive female developer to walk alongside her instead.

Book Outline

In the following chapters of this book, we explore how culture affects leadership (chapters 2 and 3) and the relationship between disciples and leaders (chapter 4). We emphasize the importance of identifying *all* leaders, not just more prominent ones, providing an overview of different types of leaders (chapter 5).

Chapters 6 to 11 examine biblical principles for good leadership and discuss their expression in different cultural contexts. Having outlined what we are trying to develop, we then turn our attention to how best to develop it (chapters 12 to 14).

Our aim is to develop an intentional process that helps leaders become more like Jesus, grow their communities, and—together with their communities—pursue God's purpose for those communities. We want to facilitate culturally relevant approaches to leadership that nurture the entire community of believers and enable the church to flourish.

---

9 This name, along with others throughout the book, has been changed to protect the identity of the person involved.

CHAPTER

2

VALUE CULTURAL DIFFERENCE

Understand How Culture Affects Leadership

Leadership is practiced and thought about differently in different parts of the world. In Russia and North America, for example, people prefer leaders who take charge and are highly visible and assertive. In Norway and The Netherlands, people prefer leaders who are much less visible and assertive, and who work behind the scenes.[1]

The concepts of ethnicity and culture have been the subject of intense reevaluation in recent years. But experts in anthropology and missiology assure us they are vital in helping us understand why people do what they do.[2] Cultural values, ideas, beliefs and assumptions impact leadership in each part of the world.

We are all immersed in culture from before we are born until after we die. It is deeply embedded in who we are. It is an integrated complex of values, ideas, beliefs, and assumptions, with their associated behaviors, shared by a group of people.[3] In today's world, we may engage with and take on aspects of several cultures. However, we link the strongest assumptions, feelings, values, and beliefs to our experience growing up. Culture is grown into our being.

> ACKNOWLEDGE HOW DEEPLY IMPORTANT CULTURE IS TO ALL OF US.

Each culture has a more superficial, easily visible level and a deeper level that is harder to see. When it comes to leadership, the most easily visible layer consists of what leaders do. This layer is like the branches and leaves of a tree, as shown in figure 1. Underpinning these observable leadership behaviors are the values, beliefs, and feelings that people from a particular culture hold about leadership. These are like the trunk of the tree in figure 1.

---
1 Steers, Sanchez-Runde, and Nardon, "Leadership in a Global Context," 479.
2 Ortner, *Anthropology and Social Theory*, 12, 50, 112, 114; Schreiter, *New Catholicity*, 49–50.
3 This definition is based on missionary anthropologist Paul Hiebert's explanation of culture as found in *Anthropological Insights for Missionaries*, 30.

At the deepest level, like the roots of a tree, are the tacit assumptions people hold about leadership. People are not usually aware of these.[4]

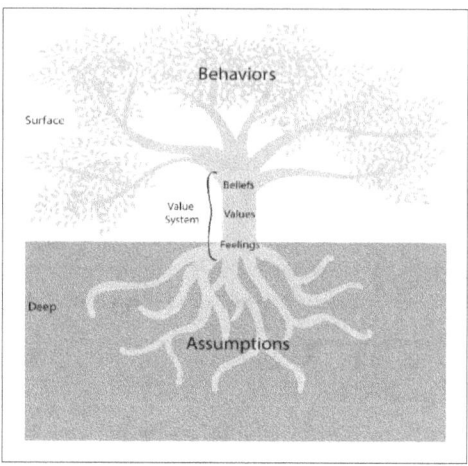

Figure 1: A model for understanding culture (adapted from Hiebert, 2008, 32–33)

Leaders who lead in a way that fits what people expect about good leadership in a specific culture are much more likely to be embraced by followers of that culture. They are also more likely to be effective as leaders.[5] It is important to realize there will be individual variation between leaders within the same culture. Nevertheless, as a group there will be a pattern of leading which is distinctive to that context. To show how leadership varies across cultures, we give examples from China, The Netherlands, and sub-Saharan Africa. This is based on research done in those settings. We then give the example of how Swedish IKEA managed the different style of leading expected in Spain.

China[6]

Chinese leaders tend to exert strong control and authority over their followers. They make decisions on their own. Being self-effacing is not viewed as positive. Their focus is to preserve the harmony and stability

---

4 The basic ideas behind this three-layer model of culture are drawn from Paul Hiebert's *Transforming Worldviews*, 32–33.
5 This reality is reflected in the findings of the first two GLOBE (Global Leadership and Organizational Behavior Effectiveness) studies on leadership, published in 2004 and 2007. Details about these studies can be found at http://globeproject.com/studies and also in printed publications. The most comprehensive reports are found in House et al., *Culture, Leadership, and Organizations*; Chhokar et al., *Culture and Leadership across the World*; House, *Strategic Leadership across Cultures*.
6 This summary is based on three sources: Gupta and Van Wart, *Leadership across the Globe*, 177; Steers, Sanchez-Runde, and Nardon, "Leadership in a Global Context," 481; Fu, Wu, and Yang, "Chinese Culture and Leadership."

of the groups they lead. In response, Chinese leaders expect respect and obedience.

The Chinese expect their leaders to be examples of morality. They must show superior integrity, be honest and trustworthy, lead by example, and not act selfishly.

Good Chinese leaders are like kind fathers. They establish and nurture good personal relationships. They look after the interests of those they lead and are sympathetic, while upholding their status as the boss. Chinese leaders care for followers' personal and family well-being. In response, followers display gratitude and loyalty.

The experience of a fired company employee illustrates the Chinese emphasis on kindness or benevolence in leaders (an aspect of *renqing*).[7] The company in this example had a policy which forbade employees from accepting any form of bribe. An employee accepted a packet of cigarettes, thinking that wasn't a big deal. But he lost his job because he had broken the policy.

A few weeks later, the man came back to the company, asking his former employer to take him back because he couldn't find a job anywhere else that would pay him as much. The company didn't let him return, because that would be against the policy. However, they made calls on his behalf and introduced him to another company.

An interviewee said, "We wanted to be humane to him because we knew he needed the money he had been making, but we also did not want to violate the rules." He added, "We are Chinese. *Renqing* is a big thing to us."[8]

The kindness and benevolence of the leaders continued even after the employee was no longer in a direct employment relationship with those leaders.

The Netherlands

In contrast to China, people in The Netherlands are much more egalitarian and skeptical about the value of leadership. They distrust strong, directive leadership. They hesitate to refer to themselves or others as leaders. The word *leader* conjures up images of Hitler and therefore implies the opposite of the democracy they value. They also don't like the practices that the word *leadership* brings to their minds. Leaders are seen as people to be suspicious of. "Terms like leader and manager carry a stigma. If a father is employed as a manager, Dutch children will not admit it to their schoolmates."[9]

---

[7] Khan, Zolkiewski, and Murphy, "Favour and Opportunity"; Fu, Wu, and Yang, "Chinese Culture and Leadership," 899.
[8] Fu, Wu, and Yang, "Chinese Culture and Leadership," 899.
[9] House, Wright, and Aditya, "Cross-Cultural Research on Organizational Leadership," 535.

A good illustration of leadership in The Netherlands is the Dutch mayor. A recent study surveyed more than two hundred Dutch mayors, interviewed some in more depth, and shadowed a few of them over four days. The researchers found that even though mayors clearly practice leadership in local government, they are not called leaders and do not call themselves leaders. Instead of following a "decide-and-accomplish" form of leadership, they deliberately do not direct about policy. Mayors see their roles as overseeing the quality of local decision-making and safeguarding the ethics and integrity of the local administration. Dutch mayors are therefore like guardians of democratic values. They guard the process of making decisions to ensure that it is fair and democratic.[10]

Sub-Saharan Africa

In sub-Saharan Africa, leadership means more than any one person. *Ubuntu* is a Bantu word used in many countries of Sub-Saharan Africa. It means that a person is only a person through or because of others. The idea is that we need other human beings to be human. The late Desmond Tutu explained *ubuntu*:

> I am because other people are. The "self-made" man or woman is really an impossibility. In Africa when you ask someone "How are you?" the reply you get is in the plural even when you are speaking to one person. A man would say, "We are well" or "We are not well." He himself may be quite well, but his grandmother is not well and so he is not well either.[11]

Since everyone is understood to be dependent on others, leaders must be welcoming, hospitable, warm, generous, and willing to share. They work to preserve harmony and advance the well-being of the groups they lead. They do this by preserving good relationships both with the living and with unseen spiritual powers. Good leaders enable others to lead in areas of their strength and expertise.

Joseph Eyong studied African leadership in twelve West and Central African communities. One of his interviewees explained how leadership is shared:

> [Leadership] is bigger than one person or the position of the appointed chief of the village because the *nfor-etok* (appointed leader) is only there as the central figure and face of the village. In our culture, everyone is involved in leadership. ... It is more about who you are in the community that matters. You can have more respect and authority than the chief.

---
10 Karsten and Hendriks, "Don't Call Me a Leader, but I Am One."
11 Tutu, *God Has a Dream*, 25.

… Some people who are wise in the cultural practices and who can communicate with the gods and spirits of our community have far more power than the leader—it is just that there must be somebody that you recognize as the general leader for many reasons but it is not that that person has more power or intelligence.[12]

Significant elements of these three different styles of leadership are all consistent with biblical values. Different cultures simply emphasize different things. Leadership is complex because it encompasses multiple relationships within and outside the group. As developers, it is good for us to be aware of these different cultural pictures of leadership. We need to be ready to take the time to learn what leadership looks like wherever the leaders we are hoping to develop live.

IKEA

When people from different cultures work together, each group expects different things of the leaders. We see this through IKEA's experience in Spain.[13] IKEA is a Swedish company.[14] IKEA's challenge was to retain its core values, including some of its management philosophy, while adjusting its leading and organizational patterns for Spain.

Swedes are highly egalitarian and individualistic, and they tolerate a relatively high amount of uncertainty. Effective leaders in Sweden encourage everyone to share in making decisions. They let people work independently. Followers and teams are empowered to take responsibility for whole areas of work.

Swedish leaders are slow to exert their power. They tend to respect and listen to each person's suggestions and take them into consideration. Dialogue and discussion are highly valued. Consensus decision-making is believed to lead to creative solutions. Swedes tend to be unemotionally practical. In conflict, they separate the person from the issue. Leaders rely on followers' and their own experience to find realistic, practical, workable solutions.

The new Spanish workers found IKEA's way of working very unnatural. They wanted to have clearly defined responsibilities and to know who was in charge of what. Spanish people expect their leaders to be more directing.

---

12 Eyong, "Indigenous African Leadership," 144.
13 This description of the case of IKEA's experience in Spain is described in T. H. Jackson, *International HRM*.
14 The following description of Swedish culture and leadership is drawn from Brodbeck, Chhokar, and House, "Culture and Leadership in 25 Societies"; Gupta and Van Wart, *Leadership across the Globe*, 216–17.

Relationships with leaders are more formal. There are clear hierarchical structures and rules in the workplace.

At the same time, they expect the atmosphere to be like a family. Leadership in Spain, compared to leadership in Sweden, is more paternalistic. In contrast to Swedes, Spaniards have a greater emphasis on people and relationships than task-fulfilment. Where Swedes approach issues in a relatively unemotional way, Spaniards are emotionally expressive. They are less likely to separate the person from the issue when they encounter conflict.

IKEA's Swedish leaders realized they needed to adapt to Spanish expectations. However, they mainly focused on exporting a Swedish way of working into the Spanish context. They selected young Spaniards for leadership whose personal values were like IKEA's. Then they trained them in "the IKEA way."

The most common way developers train leaders across cultures is like IKEA's approach. IKEA focused on setting up a Swedish business in Spain. Apart from wanting to make a profit, there was little incentive to make IKEA truly Spanish. Therefore, they selected young, malleable people to try to make them more like Swedes. In the same way, many Christian leader developers select young men to try to make them like leaders in the developers' home culture.

Adjust Our Approach according to Culture

Unlike IKEA, the church does not solely belong to any one culture. The church is a living organism. Lamin Sanneh explained that when the seed of the gospel is planted in new soil, it sprouts. The plant grows into a form which both suits the new context and transforms it, thus creating its own distinctive local character.[15] Andrew Walls called this the indigenizing principle.[16]

In fact, in any given context, the church should look like it belongs there. This means that if Jesus himself were present (and he is in his people), local people would see him as their own. In the Roma slums of Bulgaria, Jesus would be a Roma leader. In a Papua New Guinean tribe, Jesus would be a Papua New Guinean tribal leader. Instead, too often, the leaders we develop look and act like foreigners.

Our challenge as intercultural developers is how to not be like IKEA and, instead, develop leaders in ways that enable the church to flourish in

---
15 Sanneh, *Translating the Message*.
16 Walls, *Missionary Movement in Christian History*, 53–54.

its own cultural soil. This is a contextualization process. To contextualize means to allow biblical values to come to life and grow in authentic ways for each specific context.

The indigenizing principle means that diversity is normal for Christianity. The way we live out biblical principles varies from context to context across the world. Each church should be indigenous. This means its leadership should fit the patterns of the local culture. Our role as developers is to nurture indigenous patterns of leadership. These should express biblical principles in ways fitting for each cultural context. Local people should recognize leaders as *their* leaders, rather than as foreign.

If we develop leaders in our own cultural image, we run the risk of their leadership not being accepted. It may even be damaging to the church in that context. For example, all cultures have ways of supporting their leaders and holding them accountable. If we are not aware of this, we may select leaders whom the community does not recognize. We then make them vulnerable in multiple ways, including moral failure, due to lack of community support. Doing this also communicates to the surrounding non-Christian community that the church does not respect local values. It makes the church feel foreign. Even if people are attracted to Jesus, they may reject a foreign church.

> DEVELOP LEADERS IN SUCH A WAY THAT CHURCHES FLOURISH IN THEIR OWN CULTURAL CONTEXTS.

Some characteristics of leadership are widely recognized. But how these are expressed varies from culture to culture. The GLOBE project involved fifteen years of work, two hundred researchers, and thousands of surveys, as well as hundreds of interviews with middle managers in sixty-two countries.[17] This research into leadership found that in every one of the sixty-two countries it examined, people said that several qualities are important for effective leadership. These are:

1. *Charismatic leadership*, which includes (a) the ability to inspire and motivate followers with a desirable and realistic vision, and (b) being a person of integrity. These qualities match closely with Clarity and Character in our 4C model. (The 4C model is explained in chapters 6 to 10.)

---

17 The GLOBE study of leadership led to three printed publications, in 2004, 2007, and 2014, which reported on their findings. These are also summarized on GLOBE's helpful website: http://globeproject.com/studies.

2. *Team-oriented leadership*, which means that leaders (a) support those who work with them and care for the welfare of their team members. They (b) effectively build healthy communities (teams, in the GLOBE study) with a common purpose.[18] These qualities closely match with Care, Community, and Clarity in the 4C model.

In this chapter we have looked more generally at how culture affects leadership. We have shown that we cannot assume that our way of doing leadership is the only, or best, way. In chapter 3 we look at some specific dimensions of cultural difference that affect leadership.

---

18 House, *Strategic Leadership across Cultures*, 57.

CHAPTER

3

INVESTIGATE LEADERSHIP DIMENSIONS OF CULTURE

When we first started church planting in Bulgaria, just after the fall of communism, we had many short-term teams from the West come to visit us. We worked with a Turkish-speaking Muslim people group who called themselves the Millet. Our Western visitors would go into the Millet slum to meet people who they often invited to church meetings. The people would almost always reply, "Yes, we will come," but they rarely turned up. This invariably made the Western visitors very angry. They judged the Millet as inveterate liars.

The Westerners' strong negative emotional reaction was caused by a clash of cultural values. To the Millet, the *way* the words were said clearly communicated they would not come. However, the Westerners focused on the words alone. This reaction created barriers to relationship-building between the Westerners and the Millet. The only way to overcome this reaction was through intercultural training. Intercultural training gives us frameworks that help us understand cultural difference.

Frameworks are tools which help us make sense of the misunderstandings, conflicts, and confusion that occur when people from different cultural backgrounds interact. Geert Hofstede researched IBM employees across the world. Through his research, he created the most frequently used framework for discussing cultural difference.[1] Some people object to using frameworks to analyze culture because they think that doing so overly simplifies characteristics of culture. We have to balance using frameworks with recognizing that culture is a complex, constantly changing phenomenon.

Frameworks for appreciating cultural difference help us to see our own cultural bias. Otherwise, we assume that our own way of doing things is the

---
1 Hofstede, Hofstede, and Minkov, *Cultures and Organizations*.

right and only way. This is called ethnocentrism. Ethnocentrism causes us to be quick to judge. Experiencing cultural difference can result in negative emotional reactions that can be difficult to control. Intercultural training and experience help us to recognize these reactions for what they are. It makes us better at reserving judgment until we better understand what we are facing.

Although individuals within a particular culture vary in how strongly they express a cultural dimension, there can be a distinct difference between cultures. The whole group trends toward a specific way of doing things. Different cultural groups can overlap. Sometimes they will be radically different.

Erin Meyer illustrates this by giving the example of what she calls "The Scheduling Scale." Meyer asked individual business leaders how important it is to be organized (versus flexible). She found various responses. For each culture, however, most responses cluster around a single area. The variation among individual responses looks roughly like a bell curve. The majority of responses fall around the hump. Figure 2 shows the approximate positions of Germany, France, and India on Meyer's Scheduling Scale.[2]

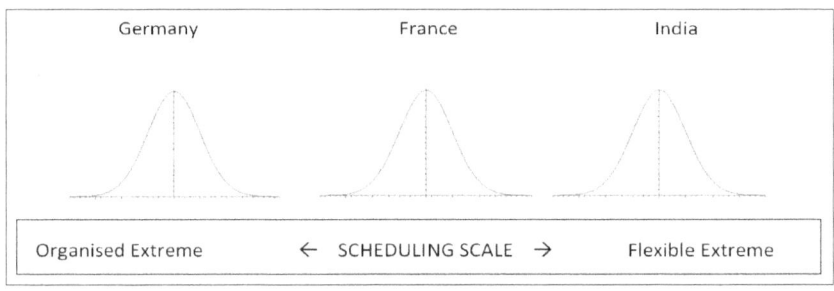

Figure 2: Variation between and within cultures in scheduling (Organized vs. Flexible)

There are five broad dimensions of culture particularly relevant to leadership. These are:

Large power distance	Small power distance
Strong patronage expectation	Weak patronage expectation
High uncertainty avoidance	Low uncertainty avoidance
High orientation to context	Low orientation to context
Strong group orientation	Weak group orientation

---

2 These insights are drawn from Erin Meyer, *Culture Map*, 116–18.

We make sense of each spectrum by comparing it with where we think our home culture lies.

In the rest of this chapter, we describe these five dimensions of culture and explain how they relate to leadership. We discuss how each affects how we develop leaders. Before starting to develop leaders, we should do some research about these dimensions in the local culture.

Gauge Power Distance

Power distance refers to the degree to which followers expect their leaders to have more power than they themselves do.[3] Different cultures are comfortable with different amounts of power distance. In an extensive study of business leaders from forty-seven nations, middle managers explained the ways they handled work events. Those from larger power-distance cultures were much more likely to rely on their superiors for guidance. Those from smaller power-distance cultures relied more on their own experience and consulting those under them.[4]

People from cultures where there is a large power distance between leaders and followers usually expect leaders to be directive. They want and expect more guidance in how to do what they are told to do. They are typically comfortable with people in authority making decisions on their behalf. If they disagree with those decisions, they are unlikely to approach their leaders directly or to contradict them to their face.

Where there is only a small power distance between leaders and followers, people expect a more equal relationship with their leaders. They like to think of their leaders as friends. They more readily approach and sometimes even contradict their bosses. They expect leaders to include them in decision-making and to be able to negotiate what they do. Leaders, in turn, tend to involve followers in decision-making and consult them more than they do in large power-distance cultures.[5]

Ulrich Jepsen's experience, described by Meyer, shows the very different expectations that people from large and small power-distance cultures have of leaders. Jepsen was a Danish business executive. In Denmark, Jepsen took pains to dress just as casually as the members of his team. Everybody called the leaders by their first name. In fact, the leader was "just one of the

---

[3] This is another way of saying how Geert Hofstede describes power distance on his website, https://geerthofstede.com/culture-geert-hofstede-gert-jan-hofstede/6d-model-of-national-culture/.

[4] Aycan, "Cross-Cultural Approaches to Leadership," 229–30.

[5] Power distance is explained in more detail in Hofstede, Hofstede, and Minkov, *Cultures and Organizations*, 53–86.

guys, just two small steps up from the janitor." Jepsen didn't have his own office, but worked in an open space with the rest of the staff.

In contrast, when Jepsen was sent to lead a team in Russia, he found that Russians called him "Mr President." They deferred to his opinions and were reluctant to take initiative without his approval. They treated him like a king. But his Russian team members complained that Jepsen was a weak, ineffective, and incompetent leader who did not know how to manage.[6]

In small power-distance cultures, where everyone is more equal, power is earned through individual achievement. Younger people are thought to have more potential for achievement. This is a major contrast to those cultures which give power to leaders according to role or age, regardless of individual achievements. For example, in sub-Saharan Africa, older people are made leaders. The community believes their life experience enables them to pass on the knowledge, skills, and types of behavior needed by the community.[7]

Power comes with honor because of the influence and status that people give leaders. In small power-distance cultures, where people treat each other equally, little honor is associated with being a leader. However, the more individual leaders achieve, the more influence and honor they receive. In contrast, in large power-distance cultures, influence and status is associated with the leadership position before the leader does anything. That is, leaders are automatically given more honor than leaders in small power-distance cultures.

Developers from small power-distance cultures who work in cultures where there is large power distance often try to stop people from honoring their leaders. This undermines the way the community naturally interacts with its leaders. Veteran missionary Julyan Lidstone writes:

> Westerners working in Asia or Africa often feel embarrassed when they are honored with public displays of deference. ... Sometimes Western Christians react against this by refusing to accept the honor, thinking that they are modelling servant leadership—but all they achieve is to cause confusion and even give offence.[8]

Teachers, like leaders, receive more honor in large power-distance settings. In these cultures, teachers dress more formally. Students address

---

[6] Meyer, *Culture Map*, 116–18.
[7] Fordjor et al., "Review of Traditional Ghanaian and Western Philosophies"; Malunga, "Learning Leadership Development from African Cultures."
[8] Lidstone, *Give Up the Purple*, 82.

them with titles of respect. Students also treat them with more respect than in small power-distance cultures. For example, in China—a country characterized by large power distance—it is disrespectful for learners to interrupt teachers to ask questions when they are teaching. Instead, Chinese learners ask questions after the teacher has finished speaking and after they have first mastered the material they have been taught. Learners are loyal, respectful, and attentive to their teachers.[9] Leaders in these contexts will treat developers like leaders and teachers. Developers, in turn, should respect these cultural norms.

Cultural expectations affect people's opinion about the credibility of teachers and their willingness to learn from them. If, as developers, we are uncomfortable with the power distance in the leaders' culture, we often try to change it. For example, developers from small power-distance cultures may try to force large power-distance leaders not to use titles and to interrupt teachers with questions. If we go too far, we create an obstacle to leaders hearing and accepting what we say. It may even result in their reacting against us. This then undermines their willingness to learn from us.

> NAVIGATE CULTURAL DIFFERENCES THROUGH STRONG PERSONAL RELATIONSHIPS.

Thankfully, leaders are generally forgiving of expatriate developers' mistakes. If we have strong personal relationships with leaders, we will be more able to navigate cultural differences together successfully. A dimension of culture that often affects the leader-developer relationship is patronage.

Research Paternalistic Expectations

Patronage is a social contract. Leaders and followers have a mutual understanding about what leaders should do and what followers will give. A good patron is like a benevolent king. A rich ruler manages his plentiful resources justly for the sake of his people. People happily give to the king and serve him, confident that he, in turn, will serve them well. The king is the patron and his subjects are his clients. This benevolent patron is like a father. He is paternalistic in a good way. He has say over clients' lives more broadly than just any work they do for him.

---

9 Watkins, "Learning and Teaching," 168; Greenlee and Stuck, "Individualist Educators in a Collectivist Society," 496.

Paternalistic leadership is most common wherever the local culture has large power distance and is strongly group-oriented.[10] It is the dominant leadership style in much of the Majority World. In countries that have smaller power distance and weak group orientation—that is, North America and most countries in Northern Europe—leaders who act paternalistically are usually not appreciated. People from these cultures feel that paternalistic leadership undermines their individual autonomy and hinders their personal development.

Paternalistic leaders may be benevolent or they may exploit their followers, depending on their motivation. Benevolent patrons have genuine concern for the welfare of followers. They create a family atmosphere through providing security, protection, and guidance to followers for every part of life. They go beyond their work roles in the organization to support and protect followers. They show family-like interest in their off-the-job lives and overall well-being. Followers appreciate this as strong, caring leadership. They, in turn, show loyalty and deference to leaders, are dependable, and comply with their leaders' wishes.

In contrast, exploitative paternalistic leaders provide care only in order that followers will do what they want them to. Followers show such leaders loyalty and deference largely because otherwise the leaders might deprive them of access to critical resources.[11]

A Turkish manager living in North America explains how he misses the way his Turkish (paternalistic) managers showed care for him, even though it felt a little overwhelming at times.

> When I worked in Istanbul, I felt extremely overwhelmed by my managers' interest in my personal life. After four years of working in the U.S., I now find myself longing for that attention. American managers are disinterested and distant. They could at least ask me how my children are doing or whether I'm planning to have more. I'm not expecting a detailed discussion about my personal life, but I feel like managers here only focus on the task and not on us—the people.[12]

Patron-client relationships have the potential of being mutually edifying, satisfying, and transforming. In a healthy patron-client relation-

---

10 Our explanations in this section are taken from Gupta and Van Wart, *Leadership across the Globe*, 84; Aycan et al., "Convergence and Divergence of Paternalistic Leadership," 963. Insights about patron-client relationships in Christian ministry from Lidstone, *Give Up the Purple*, and Georges, *Ministering in Patronage Cultures*.

11 Pellegrini and Scandura, "Paternalistic Leadership: A Review and Agenda for Future Research," 573; Jackson, "Paternalistic Leadership."

12 Pellegrini and Scandura, "Paternalistic Leadership," 572.

ship there is a cycle of generous giving and grateful responding. This cycle can be a rich, trusting relationship in which cherished Christian values and attitudes flow between patron and client.[13]

The perfect patron is God himself. He has supreme authority over all people and things. He uses that authority to look after the world and its people, and to pour out his unmerited favor on those who give their loyalty to him (Ps 99:1–3; Ps 104; Eph 1:3). When Jesus had compassion on the five thousand and miraculously fed them, the crowd interpreted this in terms of patronage. They wanted to make him king by force. They thought this would assure them of a constant supply of bread (John 6:1–15, 26–27).

Many developers work with people who are used to a paternalistic style of leadership. Developers who have grown up in weak patronage cultures have to learn how to cope with the clients' expectations of patrons. Those who come from cultures with small power distance usually find being treated as a patron discomforting. Most, at first, reject being a patron and refuse its obligations.

It *feels* wrong to be given the honor of being a patron. It feels even more wrong when asked for specific benefits, such as money. They often react by distancing themselves. They try to make the clients see them as equals. The problem is that the client leaders do not understand the developers' reactions.

A missionary who had been training leaders among the Quichua in Ecuador for many years comments:

> After I saw how uncomfortable some of our students became with our equality mindset, I realized that, for their sake, I need to stay in a role that held to a higher degree of power distance in order to meet their cultural expectations.[14]

To teach and model this form of leadership, developers from small power-distance backgrounds need to make a significant adjustment to the way they show care and concern for leaders. They need to take more time to get to know leaders, their family situations, and the issues they are facing not only in their churches but in their lives as a whole. Developers from large power-distance, patron-oriented cultures will have to adjust to the lack of respect and lack of desire for extended relationship when working with leaders from small power-distance cultures.

---

13 These insights are drawn from Del Chinchen's missionary experience in Liberia, explained in "Patron-Client System."
14 Hunter, "Discipleship Training," 43.

> CULTIVATE THE DISCIPLINE OF PERSONAL REFLECTION TO HELP CONTROL NEGATIVE REACTIONS.

The greatest challenges we face when working across cultures are unexpected. Although we may have studied about cultural difference, our feelings often well up unexpectedly. As intercultural developers, learning not to react negatively and to reflect on the source of our feelings is an important personal discipline. Many unpredictable things occur that we do not understand and cannot plan for. People from some cultures are better at coping with uncertainty than others.

Determine Tolerance for Uncertainty[15]

Cultures that are more tolerant of uncertainty are more open to change and ambiguity. They have a more relaxed atmosphere. Uncertainty avoidance is "the extent to which members of a society feel threatened by ambiguous or unknown situations."[16] Cultures with less tolerance for uncertainty overcome their anxiety by making things more predictable. They do this by having many rules. These societies uphold rigid codes of belief and behavior that provide certainty and protect conformity.

The type of rules vary according to whether the culture has strong or weak group orientation. Hofstede found that in high uncertainty-avoiding countries that also have weak group orientation, such as Italy, France, and Germany, rules tend to be explicit and written down. Where group orientation is stronger, such as Peru, Turkey, and Japan, rules are more often tacit.[17] Recently, an employee of Japan's Water Bureau, a public institution, was found to be habitually taking his lunch break three minutes early. As this broke a societal code of conduct, it was considered serious enough to warrant a public apology.[18]

Uncertainty avoidance affects how much freedom is given to followers. Leaders from cultures that tolerate uncertainty easily (e.g., Sweden, Ireland) tend to value and expect resourcefulness and improvisation from followers. They are more happy with nonconformity and more encouraging of risk-

---

15 This description of uncertainty avoidance's influence on leadership is drawn from Dickson et al., "Research on Leadership in a Cross-Cultural Context," 741–47; and Mittal and Elias, "Social Power and Leadership in Cross-Cultural Context," 65.
16 Hofstede, Hofstede, and Minkov, *Cultures and Organizations*, 2134, Kindle.
17 Hofstede, Hofstede, and Minkov, 2395–97, Kindle. The following website has a very helpful fuller list of country rankings on uncertainty avoidance, as well as further explanation of this dimension: http://www.clearlycultural.com/geert-hofstede-cultural-dimensions/uncertainty-avoidance-index/.
18 "Japanese Employer Explains Lunchbreak Punishment."

taking and innovative behaviors. They value flexibility more than planning. Cultures that do not tolerate uncertainty well (e.g., Japan, Germany) are much more concerned about conformity and precision. These leaders do more controlling, planning, and focusing on details. For example, German managers do more detailed planning than Irish managers, who value less planning and more flexibility. The Irish prize flexibility to respond rapidly to changing needs, while on-time delivery is more of a priority in Germany.

In higher uncertainty-avoidance cultures, leaders and followers have a greater need for clarity about what to think and do. People from these cultures

> tend to show less inclination to get involved in novel, ill-defined, and potentially conflictual situations that push them beyond their comfort zone. They find greater comfort in rules, structure, standard procedures, functional expertise, intellectual models, predictability, and job security.[19]

They also look for firm answers to their questions—any firm answer that will resolve confusion and ambiguity. In these cultures, people are much more likely to view leaders who decide quickly without consulting followers as effective and to view a consultative approach to decision-making negatively.[20]

People from cultures with high uncertainty avoidance prefer well-structured training programs. They prefer well-defined instructions, objectives, and assignments. Teachers avoid ambiguity by doing most of the talking and by posing questions that have only one right answer. They reward accurate rather than innovative answers to problems. They discourage alternative answers. Learners expect teachers to have all the answers. Saying "I don't know" in answer to a question is unthinkable.

In contrast, people from low uncertainty-avoidance cultures are much more comfortable with unstructured learning. They can tolerate unclear objectives, broad assignments, and a lack of timetables. Questioning and innovation by students is encouraged. Teachers reward learners who find innovative solutions to problems. Teachers aren't expected to have all the answers, and it's fine for them to say "I don't know."

Developers working with leaders with a low tolerance for uncertainty need to make their expectations very clear from the start. They need to accept that these leaders will be relatively unlikely to take risks by asking questions or trying new or unfamiliar tasks. They will need more support and structure.

---
19 Hoppe, "Cross-Cultural Issues in the Development of Leaders," 354.
20 Aktas, Gelfand, and Hanges, "Cultural Tightness–Looseness and Perceptions of Effective Leadership."

Developers from high uncertainty backgrounds may well find their low uncertainty-avoidance leaders openly rebelling against their controlling style of teaching. They will have to adjust to give leaders more freedom. They will also have to manage any personal anxiety this causes.

The most common way we try to control a group we are leading is through the words we use. But we communicate more than the words we speak. Other people in the context are also communicating even if they are silent. Everything that is happening in the context is important. Cultures vary in how much attention they give to what is happening beyond the words.

PAY ATTENTION TO MORE THAN WORDS.

Pay Attention to Context

Cultures fall along a continuum for the focus they give to words versus context in communication. People from cultures highly oriented to context pay more attention to the many nonverbal cues in the context. This includes the room the communication is happening in, the ways people dress, how people are sitting or standing, the tone of voice, and gestures. They "listen" to the whole person and context rather than just the words. They "read the air" to make out the communication. A Japanese man explains,

> In Japan, we implicitly learn, as we are growing up, to communicate between the lines and to listen between the lines when others are speaking. Communicating messages without saying them directly is a deep part of our culture, so deep that we do it without even realizing it.[21]

In South Korea this ability is called *nunchi*, which means "eye measure." The ability to look at other people and correctly interpret the nonverbal cues they are giving is central to good leadership in these cultures.

Most Western cultures pay little attention to context. In these cultures, people pay attention almost exclusively to the words in communication. They give very little attention to nonverbal cues, people's postures or gestures, or to location.

People with low orientation to context believe that if people view a written document, it has been communicated. They also tend to assume that written or verbal agreements are binding and unchangeable. In contrast, for high context people, written words of agreement are starting points. They recognize that relational and contextual issues often mean that written documents have negotiable meaning.

---

21 Meyer, *Culture Map*, 33.

People from low context cultures expect leaders to be "true to their word" (written or spoken) and to do what they say they will do. Leaders listen carefully to the words followers say and hold them accountable to them. "You said you would …" is a phrase commonly heard in low context cultures.

An example of the influence of high-context communication on leadership comes from a group of Asian Christian leaders who were choosing a new leader for their mission agency. Leaders were asked if they would support a particular person as leader, and each said yes. When the potential new leader was asked what he thought, he said, "See—they really don't want me." Using nonverbal communication, the leaders in the meeting were clearly communicating "no" when they were saying "yes."[22]

Missionary acquaintances of ours who have worked many years in Papua give another example:

> In 2019 we had a meeting in the Papuan Highlands about a property that was officially owned by a church but understood by all to be run by our mission. We desired to hand the responsibility of the property back to the church. A team leader from the area decided that the best way to do this was to give responsibility for the property management over to his local friend who was a member of the church regional leadership. When we met with the immediate local church leaders of the area that the property was located they all also said yes at the meeting and agreed to appoint this man from the church regional leadership as being in charge of the property.
>
> Later the mission organization was approached by one of the national church leaders who was also present at the meeting. He said that no one at the meeting had agreed with the regional leader being appointed, despite saying yes with their mouths. It was clear to him through their posture, their countenance, the lack of discussion over the decision and other high context cultural cues that they were in fact in disagreement over the decision. The yes from their mouths was to save face to the regional church leader and to show respect to the missionary who had made the recommendation. The regional leader was not appointed as property manager.

Duane Elmer calls this a "relational yes."[23] It shows respect, values the other person, and saves from embarrassment. People use the relational yes as a way of preserving the harmony of the group when direct communication would damage relationships.

---

22 Plueddemann, *Leading across Cultures*, 77.
23 Elmer, *Cross-Cultural Conflict*, 118–20.

People with a high context orientation view one another more broadly than the words they say. Followers look at the whole picture of leaders' lives, including the circumstances and other people that might have influenced the leaders to behave in the way they did. In contrast, followers from cultures with low orientation to context tend instead to focus mainly on leaders' words (spoken and written). They give less attention to leaders' behavior, mainly looking at how well it matches the leaders' words.

Context orientation strongly affects how leaders prefer to learn. Leaders with high context orientation pay attention to the whole context of the training. Words said or read are only a small part of the context. Because of this, they learn best by watching, memorizing whole texts, informally relating to others, and taking part in activities. Leaders raised in low context cultures tend to be strongly verbal and analytical in their approach to learning. They expect to learn by reading, asking questions, and by breaking texts down into parts.[24]

Leadership development in cultures with low orientation to context usually uses lectures and written texts. The words of the lectures and texts are separated from everyday experience by using more abstract, formal language. The settings for learning (e.g., classrooms) are also set apart from the rest of life. This promotes talking about ideas just for the sake of those ideas, which is highly characteristic of Western theological education.

Peter Chang likens the Western approach to a Western meal of separated items like steak, potatoes, and peas. He contrasts this with high context-oriented learning, which is more like a Chinese chop suey, Korean bibimbap, or a Thai noodle dish. These dishes mix all the ingredients together.[25] Both high-context and low-context orientation leaders can benefit from each other's ways of learning. Developers need to balance leaders' preferred way of learning with the benefits of extending the way each group engages with their context.

It isn't surprising that we often find high-context orientation and high-group orientation together. A major part of communication is the surrounding people. Although communication is essential for groups, groups are much more complex than this. Groups provide us with identity, and obligations toward those we identify with.

---

24 More information about field dependence (high context) and independence (low context) can be found in the chapter on "Intelligence and Learning Styles" in Lingenfelter and Lingenfelter, *Teaching Cross-Culturally*; and Pithers, "Cognitive Learning Style."
25 Chang, "Steak, Potatoes, Peas and Chopsuey."

Look at Groups

People from cultures with strong group orientation are highly loyal to the groups they belong to. This includes their extended family and other groups, like church. The needs, desires, and goals of their groups are often more important than their individual goals. They make decisions by considering what will be best for their group.

People with weak group orientation, in contrast, define their identity much more independently. They make decisions based on what will be best for them as individuals. They prioritize personal rather than group goals. They aim for personal achievement and individual rights. They exercise much more freedom in choosing which groups to be part of.

Two groups of Chinese and two groups of North American management trainees demonstrated different group orientation well. Participants in all four groups were given a set of forty small tasks to complete. Researchers told one Chinese and one American group to complete as many tasks as they could. The researchers said they would measure their performance *as a group*. The remaining two groups—one Chinese and one American—were told to complete as many tasks as possible *as individuals*. Also, the researchers told half of the participants in each group to work anonymously and the other half to write their names on their worksheets.

The Chinese participants worked much better when they knew their results would be anonymously recorded as a group. They performed worst when working individually and when they wrote their names on the worksheets they completed. The American participants worked best on their own and when they knew their names would be seen. They performed worst when anonymously working in a group.[26]

Jacob Wesseling contrasted the way East Asian (strong group orientation) and Westerners (weak group orientation) think about their groups. East Asians bind their personal identity with their group. In contrast, Westerners base their sense of identity on the sense of self they bring to the group. In Western groups, individuals come together to achieve a mutually accepted purpose. In East Asian groups, preserving group harmony is an end in itself (even though the group does work together to achieve its specific purpose).[27]

---

26 Earley, "Social Loafing and Collectivism."
27 Wesseling, "Culturally Conceived Systems for Healthy Groups." Wesseling bases his idea on Patrick Lencioni's model of effective teams (see *Five Dysfunctions of a Team*), which assumes team members are from a Western culture.

The descriptions of leadership most common in books about leadership are distinctive in their lack of group orientation and their focus on individual leaders. The vast majority have been written in Western business contexts and through research conducted by Western researchers. In the leadership they describe, resources, power, and honor flow upwards toward a pinnacle—an individual leader.

The most prominent examples of this are the large salaries given to successful business leaders. These leaders receive the resources of the community as personal benefits. In contrast, leaders in strongly group-oriented cultures are embedded in networked communities. Leadership is part of the group, supported by the group, for building up the group. Resources flow to the leaders, who use them for the benefit of the whole community. The community collectively owns its resources.

Weakly group-oriented education focuses on developing individuals to help them pursue their personal aims in life. Developers with weak group orientation promote these values even when working with strongly group-oriented leaders. This is because their community-excluding values are deeply ingrained. This compounds when developers also have a low context orientation. It is very difficult for them to *see* the groups.

People in more strongly group-oriented cultures share the responsibility for leaders' learning and growth for the benefit of the community. We discovered this when studying at an Australian Bible college alongside students from Singapore and Malaysia. These students were preparing to serve God, just as we were, as cross-cultural missionaries. In contrast to us, they didn't have to fund themselves. Their churches had sent them to the college and were fully funding their Bible-college training. Upon their return home, their churches expected them to serve in the church for one to two years before sending them overseas.

We, on the other hand, were coming from a much more individualistic environment. We paid for our own training. While our church was happy for us to be studying at Bible college, it did not expect us to serve in the church afterwards. Neither we, nor the church, expected the church to support us financially. The church also didn't give much input into our future after Bible college.

In the strongly group-oriented cultures of sub-Saharan Africa, leaders are nurtured to serve the community's needs, aims, and aspirations. The focus is on helping individuals understand their loyalty and place in their community. The group considers the knowledge that leaders gain to be useful only if it helps solve the whole group's problems.[28]

---

28 Malunga, "Learning Leadership Development from African Cultures," 7–8; Fordjor et al., "Review of Traditional Ghanaian and Western Philosophies."

The Bible strongly affirms that learning, like any resource, belongs to the community and should always be passed on (e.g., 2 Tim 2:2). Leadership development should intentionally include passing on any learning to the community. We should also evaluate what we do for continuing community benefit.

> INSTILL A 2 TIMOTHY 2:2 HABIT OF ALWAYS PASSING ON LEARNING.

Western education promotes competition for individual success. This results in students hating group work because they see it as negatively affecting their individual results. This ethos of individual competition directly opposes the biblical value of building one another up and intentionally working for their best interests (Matt 7:12; Eph 4:11–13). The Millet gave us a good lesson on this.

We used to run three-month training schools for Christian leaders and emerging leaders. Toward the end of one of these, I (Richard) organized a final exam. (Our thinking about exams has definitely changed since then!) When I received the exam papers, it was immediately clear that one participant had copied his answers from another. The next morning, I went to that student and told him that we could not in good conscience let him pass the training course because he had cheated.

That afternoon the unofficial leader and spokesperson of the group of trainees came to my house. He told me in no uncertain terms that I could not fail the student. "Either the whole group passes and graduates together, or none of us graduate," he explained.

As I talked further with the group, it became clear they believed that those who knew the answers should help those who did not. This ensured that they all progressed through the course together, learning from one another.

Instead of training toward independence, the goal of Christian leadership development should be to increase leaders' interdependence with followers. People with weak group orientation have much to learn about this. Koreans, for example, believe that a person becoming independent of their community is immature or self-centered.[29] On the other hand, strongly group-oriented developers working with leaders who are weak in group orientation will need to find a balance between biblical communal values and individualist expectations.

---

29 Nah, "Can a Self-Directed Learner Be Independent?" 18.

Explore Group Influence on Individuals

Every community confers honor on its leaders. Honoring or shaming leaders is one way that a community can give them feedback about their behavior and attitudes. Followers of Jesus are taught, "Honor those who are your leaders in the Lord's work. … Show them great respect and wholehearted love because of their work" (1 Thess 5:12–13). But the ways groups honor or shame leaders vary from culture to culture.

Where group orientation is strong, the honor of individuals, families, or even communities is highly dependent on how the rest of the group views those people. One expression of this is "face." Face is a way of talking about how people appear before their community. In these groups, people are continually thinking about what they do according to how surrounding people will see it.

The Millet are constantly concerned about personal and family standing before the community. They weigh potential actions in relation to what the community will see and gossip about. They are concerned about whether what they do will preserve their honor or shame them.

Another good illustration of this is the Danish example we wrote about in the "Gauge Power Distance" section. Following his success working in an open office among his staff in Denmark, Jepsen gave up his prestigious corner office in Russia. This was damaging to his leadership, however, as the Russian team members felt that he was signaling to the company that their team wasn't important.[30]

In the Japanese Water Bureau example in the "Determine Tolerance for Uncertainty" section, breaking the rules reflected badly on the whole organization. The top leaders of the Water Bureau had to admit the fault and apologize for it before all Japanese society. Thus they gave a televised press conference in which they expressed deep regret for the employee's behavior and gave a public bow as a sign of apology.[31]

In cultures with weak group orientation, people are socialized to determine individually what they should do, with little regard for others' opinions. Although they may have some concern about how others see them, the value placed on this is less than other factors, such as achieving individual, personal goals. Anglo-Australians, who have small power distance, give minimal honor to their leaders. Yet they still use shame as a way of attempting to control their leaders' actions or attitudes.

---

30 Meyer, *Culture Map*, 116–18.
31 "Japanese Employer Explains Lunchbreak Punishment."

The community expresses its displeasure publicly through news reporting or social media. The impact of honor or shame is offset by individuals' sense of personal worth and ability to explain their actions to the group.

It is important for us, as developers, to understand how honor and shame "works" in the particular cultural context in which we serve. This means learning how to give honor to leaders in ways that local people recognize. It means embracing rather than resisting honor when it is given to us. When honor is given, we should take time to learn what it means. This includes learning what people do that brings them honor and how they should respond to the group.

Learners from strongly group-oriented cultures where group harmony is a high priority will tend not to do anything that will cause themselves, or others in the learning group, to lose face. They will not speak up or ask questions in the whole group, but are usually comfortable expressing their opinion in small groups. This means that it is very important that developers avoid situations that might cause leaders to lose face in front of the group. Care should be taken to avoid singling people out, especially for criticism, in front of the group. It is better to address any shortcomings or areas that need improvement either in one-on-one conversations or to the whole group in a general way. Using indirect forms of communication may also help to preserve the face of group members and the harmony of the whole group.

It isn't possible to recommend a single way of teaching and correcting (2 Tim 3:16) that will work in every cultural context. We can research how local people use honor and fear of shame to motivate one another. Christopher Flanders reminds us that in the Bible "dangling the carrot of honor and holding the threat of shame are dominant forms of motivation, positive and negative, prescriptive and proscriptive."[32] Since this is the case, we should learn how to use honor and shame sensitively to motivate leaders toward God-honoring actions and attitudes.

Learn with Humility

Leadership is a multifaceted set of behaviors. Many ingredients make up any particular culture's preferred pattern of leadership. It can take many years for developers to be able to understand and fully appreciate a particular culture's preferred pattern of leadership. A helpful starting point is to identify a few ingredients of the leadership mix that differ between the culture of leaders and our own home culture. This can help us to offset

---

32 Flanders, "Honor and Shame," 89.

our ethnocentric assumption that our own way is the only or the best way of leading. We need to be ready to invest the time necessary to learn the culture of the leaders we hope to develop.

Along the spectrum of each cultural dimension, there is no ideal Christian position. Sin affects all the dimensions. Each dimension, throughout its range, has positive elements that can be lived out in God-honoring ways.

Take power distance, for example. From the Bible's point of view, neither large nor small power distance is definitively better. Several New Testament passages support large power-distance values. Examples include Peter telling younger believers to submit to their elders (1 Pet 5:5) and the command in Hebrews to submit to one's spiritual leaders (Heb 13:17). In larger power distance contexts, people submit to those in power without questioning their decisions. They respect the authority of the position entrusted to the leaders by the community.

The Bible also gives examples of small power distance. In smaller power distance contexts, people consider themselves peers of leaders and therefore able to question and criticize them. Jesus often emphasized the equality of status of people under God. Jesus criticized the Pharisees who flaunted their authority and loved to have the places of importance and honor (Matt 23:5–11). Jesus also criticized his disciples when they argued over who would be the greatest among them (Matt 20:25–28). Paul intentionally decreased the power distance between himself and the Corinthians by explaining that he came to them in weakness and with great fear and trembling. He tried to win back their loyalty with persuasion rather than asserting his power over them (1 Cor 2:2–5; 2 Cor 1:24).

The Bible consistently highlights the dangers of pride (e.g., 1 Tim 3:6; Matt 23). Even a tiny power distance gives leaders influence over others and the opportunity to receive benefits not of their own making. This influence and receiving of benefits can tempt leaders to consider themselves better than others. Whether the power distance between followers and leaders is small or great, any leader is prone to pride. As James Plueddemann reminds us,

> The Bible stands in judgment of arrogant leadership in every culture. Scripture seems to leave room for some flexibility regarding power distance in leadership style but not in leadership attitudes. The heart of every leader must be humble, seeking the good of others and suspicious of one's own motives.[33]

---
33 Plueddemann, *Leading across Cultures*, 103.

Developers must also be humble. Humility helps us to overcome our ethnocentrism and be open to learn. It reminds us that we too are disciples, walking together with leaders on the Jesus Road.

In chapters 2 and 3 we have focused on the cultural characteristics of leadership. In chapter 4 we step back and consider the similarities and relationship between leaders and followers in churches.

CHAPTER 4

DISCIPLE LEADERS LIKE ALL OTHER DISCIPLES

All Christian leaders are disciples. All believers should be intentionally helped to grow in Christ by more mature believers and peers who walk alongside them. Failures of leadership are more often because of discipling problems than leadership-development issues. The Lausanne Movement's Cape Town Commitment highlights this problem:

> The rapid growth of the Church in so many places remains shallow and vulnerable, partly because of the lack of discipled leaders, and partly because so many use their positions for worldly power, arrogant status or personal enrichment. As a result, God's people suffer, Christ is dishonored, and gospel mission is undermined.[1]

Discipling leaders is the same as for all believers. Leaders are integral members of their communities. They share the same culture and discipling issues. We don't focus on how to disciple across cultures in this book; our book on intercultural discipling explains how to do this.[2]

Ideally, leaders are not new believers (1 Tim 3:6). Leaders need to have had time to grow as disciples and for their faith and character to be tested. Paul warns Timothy that new believers are more at risk of failure as leaders due to pride. In the same way, the community needs time to see whether the leaders' transformation is lasting. It wants proof that leaders' faith is resilient in the face of the temptations and stresses of normal life. If a new believer is already someone of good standing in the community, like Cornelius (Acts 10:22), people around them will be more confident of their leadership as Christians.

Sometimes, especially when churches are growing rapidly, people become leaders when they are very new disciples. Often, new believers

---
[1] Lausanne Movement, "Cape Town Commitment."
[2] Hibbert and Hibbert, *Walking Together on the Jesus Road*.

convert out of behavior which the whole community condemns. In the early 1990s, Millet men often became leaders after being believers for only a few weeks. They came out of an atheistic and Islamic background, complicated by poverty, alcoholism, and domestic violence. They had minimal knowledge of Christianity. There were no mature male believers who could act as examples or mentors for these new leaders. The Christian and non-Christian community was suspicious of them until they had proven their transformation over a longer period. Disciples need time to be tested in real life. Then the whole community can be confident that they are good examples of Christian living.

When people become leaders before they are ready, it is important to recognize that these leaders fulfilled a need that was thrust on them. This might occur where the church is growing rapidly or where missionaries doing pioneer church planting have to leave due to circumstances outside their control. Sometimes there are cultural causes. For the Millet, which is a highly gendered culture, as soon as men became believers, the women handed over leadership of the churches to them. Although these leaders needed to be developed, the main issue was not leadership development. They needed to be discipled. These leaders could not be examples or disciple others because no one had discipled them. Developers' role in situations like this is to facilitate discipling for the *whole* church. This is the foundation for effective leadership development.

> DISCIPLE LEADERS IN THE SAME WAY AS ALL DISCIPLES.

In these situations, developers often separate out leaders for their own special discipleship program. They focus on the faults of these new-believer leaders and set up a remedial discipling program to fix them up. This approach is unhelpful. The whole church needs discipling. We can trust that as each leader and church member grows in Christ, the Holy Spirit will work on their faults, according to his priorities.

Creating special discipling just for leaders encourages elitism, as leaders can think they are better than other disciples. It may also unintentionally communicate that only leaders need to be discipled. Some might think it is okay to create an elite because of Jesus's twelve disciples. At the start of the church, however, Jesus made clear that he was forming disciples who were expected to make more disciples just like themselves. He was consistently quick to correct the disciples' inclination to assume they were different or better than others. As pride is a particular temptation for leaders, separating them out for special discipling draws them into this temptation. It is critical for them to have a healthy perspective of themselves in relation to their siblings in Christ. If someone refuses to be discipled with "normal" Christians and wants "special" discipling, we should question their fitness for Christian leadership.

Leadership-development programs are often actually discipleship programs. This is common because people are allowed into leadership-development programs when they are new disciples or not mature enough to be leaders. Sometimes they enter a program simply because they are available (e.g., unemployed). They may speak the language of the developers or can cope with the training approach (e.g., they have some school experience). At other times, churches send people with problems they want to get fixed up. While there may be a place for this type of discipleship program, this is not the purpose of leadership development.

Test Leaders First as Disciples

Where we have the choice, we should resist accepting people for leadership development who have not proven themselves as disciples. First, their communities should approve them as exemplary disciples and leaders. We interviewed a

> GET LOCAL BELIEVERS TO IDENTIFY EXEMPLARY DISCIPLES.

missionary who was serving in West Africa among a traditionally Muslim people group in which several thousand people had become Christ-followers. He explained that the small Bible school he taught at had been created to train leaders for this group. But at least half of those chosen for training were young men with multiple basic problems in their lives—problems that would be addressed in discipling. Churches hoped that the Bible school would disciple them. Even after three or four years, in this missionary's estimation, a good proportion were not suitable people to lead churches.

As we gained more experience in developing leaders in Bulgaria, we put more time and effort into the careful selection of people for three-month residential schools. This enabled us to focus more of our time on working to nurture the distinctives of leadership rather than discipling. This did not mean, of course, that we ignored modeling and teaching basic aspects of being a disciple of Christ. But we had more confidence that the men and women we were training already had a lot of experience being disciples. They could resolve conflicts among themselves and were able to work together well. As part of our selection process, we spent more and more time visiting and speaking with potential trainees' home churches.

The believers in leaders' churches are the best people to determine who the most exemplary disciples are. As developers coming from outside the local context, it is very difficult for us to be sure what exemplary disciples look like. If they interact with us outside their homes or apart from other local community members, their behavior may be quite different than when we are not there. Many things in the local culture will be different than what we are used to. It is normal to judge people by our own familiar standards. However, different cultures can express the same standards very differently.

For example, being hospitable is a key biblical requirement for leaders (1 Tim 3:2). For Anglo-Australians, being hospitable means smiling at visitors to a meeting and possibly offering them a cup of tea. For the Millet, being hospitable means opening their home, spending much time with any visitor, going into debt to feed them lavishly, and insisting on their staying for many hours or even days.

The Millet would definitely fail most Anglo-Australian leaders by this standard. Conversely, Anglo-Australians judging Millet Christian leaders regarding being hospitable might well pass people who local Millet would never consider hospitable. The more time we spend with people in their homes and communities, the more we will appreciate local standards. The more we build relationships with local people, the more they will feel free to be honest with us. We are also more likely to be ready to hear what they have to say.

Identify Exemplary Disciples

The whole of leaders' lives should bring honor to the Lord. They exemplify for followers what living for Christ amid day-to-day life in their community means. Both believers and nonbelievers should be able to point to them as good examples of what it means to follow Jesus. Daunting though it may be, the Christian leader should be able to say, "Imitate me, just as I imitate Christ" (1 Cor 11:1). When believers wonder what to do in particular situations, they consider similar situations faced by their leaders and use that consideration as a starting point for action. Leaders therefore act as living references for other believers.

Leaders are examples through the way they live out their daily life. Good leaders have and are growing in qualities of Christian character. Paul and Peter describe what church elders and deacons should be like in 1 Timothy 3:1–13, Titus 1:5–9, and 1 Peter 5:1–4. These qualities are not exclusive to leaders, but are what Paul and Peter consider leaders should display. The focus of each of these descriptions is the character of the leader. They highlight self-control, self-discipline, devotion to God, gentleness, humility, faithfulness, integrity, and honesty.

Although all leaders should be exemplary disciples, not all exemplary disciples will be leaders. Some exemplary disciples will have gifts in other areas. A good example of this is Dorcas (Acts 9:36–42). Dorcas was obviously an exemplary disciple. Her community appreciated her deeply. However, there is no suggestion that she was a leader of that community. Her gifting was in service. This means that leaders will not be the only exemplary disciples in a church. Leaders are not an exclusive group of "super-Christians."

One major thing that all disciples learn is what to do when they sin and fail. Sometimes people think an exemplary disciple is perfect. This is not the case. The example is in being quick to admit sin and to repent. The same principle applies to failure. We all fail continually. Learning how to cope with our failures and grow through them develops our resilience. If leaders are transparent about sin and failure, this reassures followers about their own human failings. It provides them with an example of a path to growth through failure. Transparency in this area also protects leaders from pride.

Foster Continuing Growth

We all continue to grow as disciples throughout our lives. We continue to learn from Jesus, becoming more like him as the Holy Spirit transforms us day by day (Matt 11:29; Rom 8:29; Phil 1:6; 2 Cor 3:18). We grow in putting Jesus first in our lives (Luke 14:25–26; Matt 16:24) and responding to God's Word (John 8:31; Acts 2:42). We grow in our relationship with God (John 15:5–8; Col 1:9–10) and people (John 13:34–36; Eph 5:1–2). We display the fruit of the Spirit (John 15:5–27; Gal 5:22–23; Col 1:10) and make more disciples (Matt 28:19).

Continuing growth in Christ helps protect leaders against their vulnerability to pride and abuse of power. As part of discipling a whole group of believers, we should help them strengthen local church systems which support leaders in their ongoing growth. These structures hold them accountable as disciples of Jesus, and also as leaders. These systems usually involve a group of peers who have the right to challenge leaders' attitudes and actions.

> STRENGTHEN LOCAL CHURCH SYSTEMS TO HELP LEADERS CONTINUE TO GROW.

At the same time, it is also wise to encourage groups to set up culturally fitting ways of managing money and resources. Systems like this remind both followers and leaders that they are, together, disciples of Jesus. They help guard against leaders considering themselves better than other disciples. As much as we can, we should help leaders to value their community's role in helping them continue to grow.

Rather than being superhumans, Christian leaders are disciples in a community of disciples. They grow together with the whole community of disciples. They face challenges with the group they lead. Along with other disciples, they learn through conflict. Like all other disciples, leaders grow, make mistakes, fail, recover, and repent. As Ash Seaton remarks, good leaders do not hesitate "to embrace the refining process of being in community with fellow disciples." They model for their community what it looks like to "walk this refining process together."[3]

Leaders' own communities are the best context to evaluate their gifting. One part of discipleship is to help disciples discover their gifts and learn to use them to build up the body of Christ. Disciples should be encouraged to experiment with different ministry options, including leadership. If they do this in their local church, church members will be able to tell whether they have a gift of leadership. Church members can support them in working out whether failure means they need to work harder, develop their skills more, or should try something else. Church members can also evaluate whether what disciples do in church contexts matches what happens in their homes. As developers, we should empower churches to evaluate and support leaders as disciples.

Remember That We Are Also Disciples

As developers, let us always remember that we too are disciples, equal to church members. Just as leaders are examples for their followers, developers are examples for the leaders we develop. Developers are not better or greater than leaders. We all make mistakes. We are all continuously learning and growing in our faith. We can all learn from each other. Humility and mutual respect are the bedrock for effective leadership development.

Our attitudes and actions are on display as we live out the Bible alongside the leaders we are developing. It is helpful to discipline ourselves to reflect continually on our attitudes, thoughts, actions, and interactions. This helps us to be aware of what we are passing on as living examples.

---
3 Seaton, "Lunch with Ash," 416–25, Kindle.

Too often we think only about the content we teach. Learning to see and reflect on ourselves in context, and listening to the people around us, will help us to grow as developers. We need to be conscious of what we are modeling. Our model will be reproduced through many generations of disciples.

> CONSCIOUSLY MODEL WHAT YOU WANT TO REPRODUCE.

In this chapter, we have focused on the similarities between leaders and disciples. In one sense, there is no difference, because all leaders are disciples. On the other hand, we know that leaders are important and that they are needed. Leaders are, firstly, disciples. On that foundation, they grow as leaders.

In discussing leaders' development, we assume they are being or have been discipled. At the same time, even if leaders are very mature believers, we do not assume they are perfect, just as we also are not perfect. We all keep growing in Christ until the day we go to be with him. In chapter 5 we consider how we identify all the leaders in the community of believers.

Chapter 5

Identify All the Leaders

Leadership is a gift from God to his community, the church. God gives multiple gifts to his people. Only one of these is leadership (1 Cor 12:4–31; Rom 12:6–8). It is clear from these passages that leadership is a specific ability and capacity to lead. God gives it to benefit the whole body of Christ. It is not a personal characteristic worthy of special honor. We do not personally create it. If people in a local church community recognize leadership capacity given by God by following a leader, then they are simply recognizing one of God's gifts to them as a group.

The gift of leadership is no different from any other gift, such as serving others or showing kindness. Those with a gift of leadership will have followers that gather around them, whether or not they have a formal leadership role in the church. The Holy Spirit is not limited to whom is officially appointed. Therefore, if we would like to develop leaders, we need to look for everyone who is leading, rather than merely focusing on people who have official leadership roles.

The typical stereotype of a Christian leader is that of a lone male acting as the sole provider of spiritual direction, teaching, and care for the group. This view, though, carries with it the danger of excluding others God has gifted to grow his church. It is important that, as developers, we are not so fixated on finding the one man that we fail to see the many other Spirit-gifted people who are leading.

To identify the leaders, we need to spend time in the local community, watch what is happening, and listen to discover who people are referring to. We need to try to put aside the ways we normally think about leaders or we may be slow to notice other leaders in the group. As leadership is different in different cultural contexts, we also need to be alert for patterns of leadership that are unfamiliar. Chapter 3 explains more about these different patterns of leadership.

BE ALERT FOR BIASES AND BLIND SPOTS.

Beyond cultural biases, we may have other biases that cause us not to see people who are leading others in the local community. Our biases create blind spots. They cause us not to see women, uneducated or illiterate people, or people from less prominent ethnic groups. However, these "invisible" leaders are often far more effective in their ministries than the visible leaders we quickly identify. In Bulgaria, for example, although semiliterate Millet women led the church to grow like wildfire, since men took over women have been made invisible. This pattern of women's leadership repeats throughout history.[1] If we develop *all* leaders, both women and men, perhaps movements will continue for longer.

Identify the Growing-Edge Leaders

Churches have different types of leaders. Edgar Elliston identifies five main types of Christian leaders.[2] Type 1 and Type 2 leaders are the "grassroots" leaders who lead small groups and ministries within a local church. Type 3 leaders have responsibility for a whole local church, while Type 4 leaders are responsible for a group of local church leaders or a very large urban church. Type 5 leaders have wide national or international influence.

Gary Corwin illustrates various types of leaders in the following three vignettes:

1. Juan is a farmer and the lead elder of a small village church in the high Andes. [Elliston's Type 3]
2. Gupta pastors a fast-growing urban megachurch made up of university students, diplomats, wealthy businesspeople, and the urban poor. [Elliston's Type 4]
3. Kofi teaches theology at an African seminary and is writing several articles for a new contextualized *Bible encyclopedia*. [Elliston's Type 5][3]

Even in these examples, we see how bias toward a single male over a congregation or classroom makes most leaders invisible. The faithful cell group leaders who share their faith with neighbors and workmates, and who labor to reproduce cells, is an example of Elliston's Type 1 leaders. The gifted woman evangelist, who starts multiple home groups and continually visits and supports the leaders of those groups, is an example of Elliston's Type 2 leaders.

---

1 Muir, *Women's History of the Christian Church*.
2 We have drawn mainly from Edgar Elliston's descriptions in our depictions of the five types of leaders. See Elliston's *Home Grown Leaders*, 26–35. Elliston, in turn, based his five types on Donald McGavran's descriptions of five types of leaders in a lecture given at Columbia Bible College in 1969.
3 Corwin, "Multi-Tasking Challenge of Training for Church Leadership," 144.

Small-Group Leaders (Type 1)

Type 1 leaders, together, have the greatest potential influence for growing the church. They are closest to the people in the surrounding community. They usually live close by and are interacting with followers in day-to-day life. They are typically leaders of new small house churches, cell groups or Bible study groups, Sunday school teachers, youth group leaders, catechists, and other ministry team leaders. New believers have most of their personal contact with a Type 1 leader. Although each leader leads the smallest number of people, Type 1 leaders are the growing-edge leaders of the church. They are in the community surrounding the local church. The community sees them, in all their strengths and weaknesses.

Intra-Church Leaders (Type 2)

Type 2 leaders' focus shifts from the surrounding community to the local church. Elders are prime examples of Type 2 leaders, as are coordinators who oversee multiple Sunday school groups, cell groups, or other kinds of ministry groups. Type 2 leaders are usually responsible for several Type 1 leaders. They have usually been Type 1 leaders first and may well be continuing their Type 1 leadership alongside the extra responsibilities of overseeing. The practical realities of time mean these leaders have less time to invest in their local communities.

Types 1 and 2 Together

D. R. David, reflecting on his in-depth study of Christian leadership in India, highlights the important role Type 1 and 2 leaders play in the health and growth of churches:

> The strength, health, and speed of expansion of the church will depend largely on what have become the core values of the Type 1 and 2 leaders. Are they servant-hearted, holy, sacrificial, compassionate, and prayerful? Do they believe in the necessity of evangelism? Are they free to exercise their gifts and innovate? Do they encourage others to join them in ministry as brothers and sisters, and as fellow members of the Body?[4]

Especially in rapidly growing church movements, many churches will emerge through the growth or merging of small groups. These small groups will continue to be created along the margins of the movement if Type 1 and Type 2 leaders are empowered and supported to keep starting new groups.

---

4 David, "India Leadership Study."

Pastors and Overseers (Types 3 and 4)

As the Type number increases, leaders become more focused on the institution of the church. As they become responsible for greater numbers of believers, they increasingly work on the structures to support those believers. Their primary influence narrows to the church and its structures.

Type 3 leaders are pastors of small congregations. In the Majority World, many are bi-vocational. In the West, most work full-time for their church. Their influence extends across an entire local church and they are often key people for developing Type 1 and Type 2 leaders. According to their personality and gifting, some spend time in the local community, while others focus on the members and organization of the local church.

In movements, these leaders are also very likely to be visiting smaller groups in nearby geographical areas who are wanting teaching and support. When the church is new and rapidly growing, these leaders will often be new believers who are unlikely to have had much, if any, Bible training. In Guatemala, this led to the development of Theological Education by Extension (TEE). This method of Bible training allows leaders to study without leaving their own contexts.[5]

Type 4 leaders are typically pastors of large, well-established churches who often lead a team of assistant pastors. Other Type 4 leaders include church overseers or bishops over a small region. Type 4 leaders, in contrast with Types 1–3, have usually been appointed by selection committees external to the local church (e.g. denominational boards). Sometimes, when a local church has grown very successfully, such as large Korean churches (e.g., Paul Yonggi Cho's church) or Hillsong in Australia, Type 4 leaders have grown with their churches. As their churches have grown, they have developed their own boards (or equivalents), which continue to approve leaders. Sometimes these boards can step in to remove leaders, such as occurred in the recent Willow Creek scandal in America.[6]

Type 4 leaders are more likely to have had formal theological training and to approach church leadership as a career. By career, we mean they will have invested in professional training (a degree) and expect churches (or denominations) to support them financially in full-time employment, continuing that support even into retirement. Except for a few gifted evangelists and social-justice activists, Type 4 leaders usually focus almost only on the church itself. These leaders tend to have minimal contact with non-Christians.

---

5 Carey and Harrison, "TEE in Historical Context," 101–4.
6 Shellnutt, "Willow Creek Investigation."

Supra-Church Leaders (Type 5)

Type 5 leaders serve in national or international leadership roles. Their influence is very broad, mostly indirect, and focused mainly on Christians. A leader of a large national or international parachurch agency and a professor at a Bible college or seminary who has a wide speaking or writing ministry are examples of Type 5 leaders.

Although these leaders attend local churches and may have some speaking or supervisory roles within them, their main attention is at a more abstract, across-churches, national or global level. As their work becomes less and less grounded in the local church, they sometimes forget their accountability to this basic foundation of Christ's kingdom. They tend to be selected into their positions by committees of similar peers. The committee sometimes includes other people who have a stake in their ministry. These leaders' influence varies according to how much national or international church leaders (especially Types 3 and 4) promote them. Examples of Type 5 international leaders in the past century are Desmond Tutu and John Stott.

Types 4 and 5 together

Type 4 and 5 leaders have an influence that reaches beyond a single church. However, that influence is mostly indirect. It depends on the leader's coworkers', assistants', or sub-leaders' work. Their influence occurs through public speaking, publications, recordings, and broadcasts often arranged by others. These leaders have often completed specialized training (e.g., DMin or PhD) and have good salaries.

Type 4 and 5 leaders are important for keeping church movements or denominations on course and well resourced. These leaders "are in the best position to think strategically and to see new opportunities."[7] Although most will have trained as a Type 3 leader, they benefit from specialized leadership development specific to the demands of their wider influence.

Type 1 leaders are not only essential to multiply churches, they are the vast majority of Christian leaders. Let's imagine a growing church movement of ten thousand believers meeting in two hundred churches. Something like two thousand Type 1 leaders for small groups of five to ten people, four hundred Type 2 leaders overseeing five Type 1 leaders each, and 150 Type 3 leaders are needed. Not all churches will be

FOCUS ON SMALL GROUP LEADERS.

---
7 David, "India Leadership Study."

large enough to have their own pastor (Type 3 leader). Some pastors will visit several churches. There may be several regional overseers and perhaps two or three national parachurch ministries (e.g., women's ministry across churches or a missionary sending agency), so a handful of Type 4 and 5 leaders are needed. The upside-down pyramid in figure 3 shows the proportion of each leader type. The wider the band of the pyramid, the larger the number of leaders it represents.

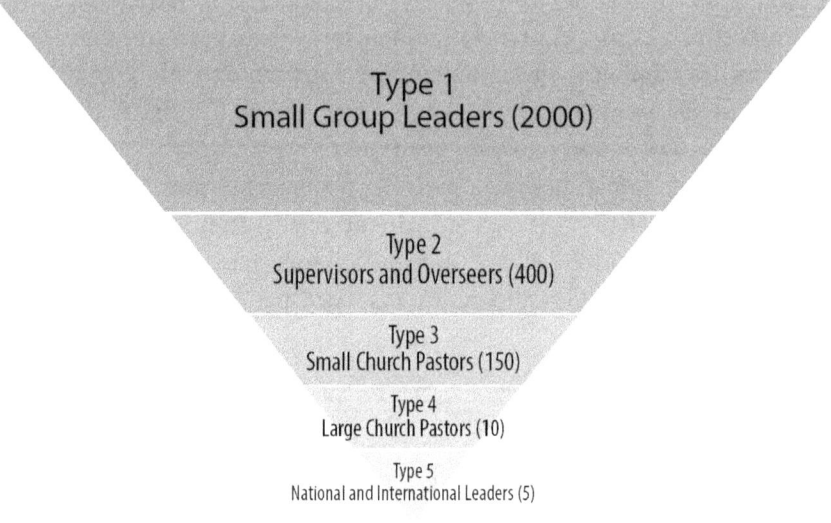

Figure 3: Leadership types and estimated number of each type in a church movement of 10,000 people

Figure 3 clearly shows many more Type 1 leaders than Type 3–5 leaders. People often assume that Type 3 leaders will develop Type 1 and 2 leaders. This often does not occur, however, because Type 3 leaders don't have the time or ability, or see the need. Millet leaders recognized the need for training for Type 1 and 2 leaders, but had not received much training themselves. This, coupled with their limited schooling, caused them to lack confidence for training people in their churches. As each leadership type emerges out of the larger group that precedes it, developing leaders in each type is an important foundation for greater leadership responsibility. Type 1 leaders lead the church's day-to-day activities and promote and oversee its growth. While leadership development should address the needs of all types of leaders, most of the effort should focus on the majority of the leaders. All too often, more attention focuses on the numerically smaller types.

Focus on the Majority

If leaders across the church or church movement have the right DNA instilled, this will reproduce itself in every new group that leaders start. This will extend into larger groups when leaders with this DNA have broader influence. In this ethos, not only do the right leaders emerge, but the whole community embodies the same values. The whole community then holds their leaders accountable for these values.

If the church already has Type 3, 4, and 5 leaders trained in theological education institutions, it will be very difficult to change the DNA of the church and leadership development to a different pattern. But we can still look for ways to develop the majority of leaders. Perhaps we can infuse new DNA from the edges.

> INSTILL REPRODUCING DNA AT THE EDGES OF THE CHURCH.

If we focus our leadership-development efforts only or mainly on preparing people to be full-time pastors of established churches (Type 3 leaders), we risk causing church stagnation and decline. Making new disciples is not these leaders' main practical priority.

Separating out people to become Type 3 leaders by giving them a special education that is not accessible to most leaders in the churches creates an elite. Elitism is problematic because it excludes most frontline leaders. It means that leaders at the center of the church institutions (Type 3–5) become out of touch with the surrounding grassroots communities that the church should be extending into.

Elitism perpetuates itself. Leaders who become part of the elite group choose people to join the group who are like themselves. Elitism often starts with good intentions. The Pharisees were an elite group who wanted to make sure that God's Law was taught correctly. But bias increasingly blinds us over time. We find it difficult to stop ourselves from privileging those who are like ourselves. We need the perspectives of people who are different from us to keep us balanced. Jesus persistently confronted this tendency and worked to develop more inclusive attitudes among his disciples.

Elitism creates a barrier between leaders who receive special training and those who don't. Type 3–5 leaders start thinking they don't need to listen to untrained Type 1–2 leaders. Leaders without the special education feel they have nothing of worth to offer. Yet it is critical for Type 3–5 leaders to listen to the perspectives of Type 1–2 leaders. This helps churches remain relevant to their surrounding communities. We can develop this by modeling attitudes that value all leaders. We can help them learn to value one another by facilitating their working together.

One Christian organization working to reach the unreached and establish churches in North India intentionally develops leaders of every type. Its work is focused on translating the Bible into multiple languages in North India and then helping people read and apply the Bible. In this setting, Type 1 leaders lead church-based Bible study groups using the new translations, groups who are learning how to read, or groups who run community-development projects. Continuing modeling, mentoring, and some formal training sessions make up most of their training.

Type 1 leaders who show an ability for wider leadership are encouraged and receive on-the-job training to serve as Type 2 leaders who coordinate several of these groups and help the Type 1 leaders. Some Type 2 leaders who show particular ability as leaders are encouraged to receive further training through intensive seminars over several years. A few have been sent to be trained in a Bible college that shares the vision for reaching the unreached, discipling, and planting churches. Graduates now serve as Type 3 pastors. They effectively oversee and support the work of many groups. Type 4 leaders are developed through mentoring and coaching.[8]

We must include the many believers who are influencing others toward Jesus in their local church and its surrounding community (Type 1–2) in leadership-development planning. If we don't develop Type 1 and 2 leaders, churches will stop reproducing. This is not an excuse to neglect Type 3–5 leaders. If we fail to develop these leaders, the churches' stability and sustainability may be compromised.

So far we have emphasized the importance of the community for leaders, including how the interaction between leaders and their communities varies between cultures. We have stressed that all leaders are continuously growing as disciples and that there are multiple leaders in churches. The majority of leaders lead small groups with members immersed in everyday life. In chapter 6 we explore the specific, distinguishing features of Christian leadership.

---

8 This information came from a conversation with senior cross-cultural workers who have been serving with this organization in North India for more than fifteen years.

Chapter 6

Foster Biblical Leadership

The Bible is the Christian's authoritative source of guidance about every facet of life, including leadership. The Bible describes and evaluates many leaders, both good and bad. As many writers on leadership point out, when we analyze all of the biblical material, it yields an unmanageably long list of characteristics.

We compared biblical teaching with research and writing on leadership, both from secular and Christian authors. This led us to identify four critical characteristics of good leadership.

Strengthen the 4 Cs—Community, Character, Clarity, Care

We have summarized these critical characteristics in four words (the 4 Cs) to make them easier to remember. These characteristics are shown in figure 4 and summarized in figure 5. Community is foundational to who Christian leaders are and what they do. Therefore we have separated it from the other three characteristics. Community is the context in which Christian leaders live out character and clarity, and promote community members caring for one another.

Figure 4: The four critical characteristics of Christian leadership (4 Cs)

Community	Leaders are inseparable from and endorsed by their communities.
Character	Leaders are growing in character qualities that reflect the character of Christ.
Clarity	Leaders have clarity about the purpose of their community and how to achieve this purpose.
Care	Leaders strengthen their whole community through enabling members to care for one another.

Figure 5: The 4 Cs of Christian leadership

Community is the context in which Christian leadership occurs. A Christian leader is not an individual in a vacuum. Without a community, or group of followers, there is no leader. Character is modeled to the community. Clarity defines the community's purpose. Care reflects the quality of interconnected relationships across the whole community. Leaders empower community members to serve one another, displaying to the surrounding world that they are followers of Jesus. These four critical characteristics (4 Cs) of Christian leadership are explored in detail in chapters 7 to 10.

Apply Biblical Metaphors Carefully

The most common biblical metaphors Christians use to describe or teach about leadership are shepherd, servant, and steward. (Steward is often translated as "manager" in modern English Bible translations.) Images are rich in complexity. That is, they are not as simple as a sentence we use to make a single point.

For example, imagine three people who come from the different places depicted in figure 6. Each person's thoughts vary about a shepherd, what the land is like, and how the shepherd herds the sheep. If we have never seen sheep, we might substitute another animal, such as pigs, which might not act much like sheep at all. If we have ever been on a sheep farm, the metaphor also evokes the sensations of that experience. The smell, heat, dirt, experience of a shearing shed, all affect our interpretation of the teaching points around the metaphor.

Jesus often used images or events for teaching, usually highlighting a single point to learn from each instance. However, we can usually find extra learning points from the richness of the picture. In John 6, Jesus evoked the image of his feeding the crowd from five loaves of bread. He created a metaphor of himself as the bread of life. He drew on the image to stress that like the Israelites needed their staple of bread to live, so we need Jesus to live eternally. But we can extend the teaching points from the image to explain

Bulgaria

USA

Australia

Figure 6: Photos of shepherds in different parts of the world

truths about how we seek out the bread of life, eat it, and share it with others.

Sometimes we can take the richness of the image too far. The more concrete thinkers in the crowd around Jesus struggled with the thought that he seemed to be suggesting cannibalism (John 6:52). This means that sometimes the limits of application of metaphors are not clear. We can see this through the continuing disagreements between Christians today. For some, eating communion bread means to be literally eating the body of Christ. For others, it is only a symbol.

Images may illustrate several different things at the same time. A good example of this is Jesus's parable of the good steward (translated as "shrewd manager" in NIV and NLT) in Luke 16:1–9. Many people struggle to accept Jesus's teaching in this parable, as he seems to promote cheating the master. However, Jesus focuses on just one aspect of what the steward did to teach a specific point: we should not love money. Rather, we should use money to gain welcome into our heavenly home. Therefore, as we apply biblical metaphors to leaders, we should be careful to highlight the points the Bible makes. We need to resist overlaying the image with added meanings based on our own experience today.

If we do make other applications from a biblical metaphor, it is good to recognize how we have arrived at those interpretations. A good example of this are the popular Western Christian images of Jesus as Shepherd. He is usually depicted in clean white robes, with perfect, fluffy, cuddly sheep, in fields of lush green grass and other vegetation. This evokes a warm, fuzzy, emotional response associated with childhood memories of safety, security, and feeling loved.

While Jesus does care for us in this all-encompassing, warm, fuzzy way, it is far from the experience of Judaean shepherds in biblical times. They had to herd their sheep because of the scarcity of pasture and water. They were constantly checking for danger from predators and thieves. David Phillips, in his encyclopedic book regarding working with nomads, comments,

> Westerners have romanticized the figure of the shepherd, so that the prevailing interpretations of the Bible passages stress such ideas as safety and comfort, rather than struggle and survival. The shepherd's life is lonely and hard, with long periods in the cold or heat, with nothing but a cloak for cover, and with only a sling and heavy stick to guard against wolves or leopards. There is the continual threat of theft of livestock, when fights can lead to injury or death.[1]

The sheep's feeling of being safe (which is, after all, a metaphor—as if sheep have human feelings) was significant because they were in constant danger from the threat of thirst, starvation, theft, or injury. Our interpretations may be valid according to the Bible generally, but they may sometimes extend beyond the meaning of what Jesus, or the biblical authors, taught through each specific metaphor.

Nurture Life in All Its Fullness

Jesus is the Good Shepherd (John 10:1–18). We know that leaders should be shepherds like him. Peter directs elders in the churches to care for their flocks, alongside a reference to the "Great Shepherd" appearing (1 Pet 5:1–4). The image of shepherd was important for Peter because this was the image that Jesus used to bring restoration and healing after Peter denied knowing him (John 21:15–17).

There is only one Good Shepherd. While leaders imitate him, they can never replace him. Some characteristics of the Good Shepherd in John 10 can only apply to Jesus. We should be careful about broadening these to apply to all leaders. For example, Jesus's sheep know his voice and follow him. While followers may know their leaders, it is Jesus's voice they should know and him they should follow. The leader's role, as one sheep among many, is to point to Jesus. Anything that leaders, as shepherds, offer, such as food for lambs (cf. John 21:15–17), comes from God. He provides it in his name, for the sake of his sheep.

> LEADERS ARE SHEEP WHO SHEPHERD GOD'S FLOCK TOWARD THE ONE GOOD SHEPHERD.

---

[1] Phillips, *Peoples on the Move*, 78.

There are other examples of shepherds who are leaders in the Bible. Two of these were major leaders of Israel: Moses and David. First, Moses tried to bring change in his own strength. He failed, and then had to spend forty years as a shepherd in the wilderness to prepare for godly leadership. It is ironic that a prince of Egypt had to become a despised shepherd to be a great leader.

We quickly learn that David was brave, courageous, and completely committed to God. Through the interactions between Saul, Samuel, Goliath, and David, we learn again that God prefers the humble shepherd who wholeheartedly follows him over human strength, outward appearance, and other human judgments of fitness. Being a shepherd, at least in Moses's and David's experience, seems to have provided these leaders with good character development in humility, courage, resilience, and complete trust in God.

The consistent message about shepherds in the Bible is that they protect the flock (Acts 20:28), watching over them (1 Pet 5:2) and feeding them (John 21:15–18). The sheep belong to Jesus, the Good Shepherd (John 10; 21:15–18; Acts 20:28; 1 Pet 2:25). In John 10, Jesus the Good Shepherd provides the supreme protection of salvation from death. The sheep and the shepherd know one another well. The sheep will not follow a stranger, which keeps them safe. The shepherd leads the sheep to nourishment, with Jesus stressing that he ensures that the sheep have a rich and satisfying life (John 10:10).

Biblical shepherds protect the flock from physical danger and death. Protection from physical danger and death includes everything necessary to nurture life—food (John 21:15–18; cf. Jude 12), water (Rev 7:7), health, and inter-sheep harmony. People often teach that protecting the sheep is chiefly about protecting doctrinal truth (cf. Acts 20:29–31). Although Jesus refers to false prophets as wolves disguised as sheep (Matt 7:15), he focuses on the actions of these people in the community of believers, rather than their preaching. Shepherds are always concerned for the whole flock of sheep. They watch over each member and note what is happening between all the sheep.

Shepherds, like stewards, manage and care for the resources of their Master, for the sake of their Master. For sheep, this means nurturing them in the fullness of life. This is so their Master can delight in them and what they produce. Leaders shepherding Jesus's sheep are expected to keep the whole flock healthy and multiplying. Keeping this perspective clarifies for leaders what their care for the community should produce.

For the sake of readers from cultures with weak group orientation, we stress that the sheep that leaders shepherd are always a flock. As a group, they are protected and nurtured into fullness of life. In Western churches, church members often expect leaders to care for each individual person, or single sheep. While this is true in a general sense, we lose sight of the flock and the need to protect and nurture it as a whole. Jesus's parable about the lost sheep (Matt 18:12–14; Luke 15:1–7) is as much about restoring it to the flock as its individual salvation. We neglect that salvation means being returned to Jesus's flock. This is in contrast to being an individual sheep in Jesus's arms (like in many pictures of Jesus as Shepherd). For strongly group-oriented Christians, the group is always present. The group is whole again when the Shepherd brings the lost sheep back.

The flock is a community. The shepherd's responsibility is to protect the community as a whole. Dangers to the community come from outside (thieves and predators), inside (wolves in sheep's clothing), or if members do not share resources fairly or start harming one another. An example of harm is unforgiveness. Jesus showed this in his parable of the unforgiving servant. This servant did not pass on the forgiveness he received from his master (Matt 18:21–35).

> LEADERS KEEP THE WHOLE FLOCK SAFE, HEALTHY, AND MULTIPLYING.

Promote One-Another Care

Leaders are servants whose master is Jesus. Serving others is for Jesus's sake. The Apostle Paul puts it this way: "You see, we don't go around preaching about ourselves. We preach that Jesus Christ is Lord, and we ourselves are your servants for Jesus' sake" (2 Cor 4:5). As servants, leaders do what is best for the people they serve rather than pandering to their own wishes, particularly for self-aggrandizement (cf. Mark 10:42–45).

Jesus used the servant image whenever disciples sought to lift themselves above others (Matt 20:28; Mark 9:33–35; 10:42–45; Luke 22:24–27). He also used it to show, in a practical way, that they should do what he did (John 13:1–17). He stressed their equal status under him—their Master, Teacher, and Lord. The image's focus is humility. Paul also invoked the image of servant to stress humility (Phil 2:3–8). And it is not surprising, therefore, that the greatest leader that Jesus supersedes was Moses, the servant of the Lord (Deut 34:5; Num 12:3; Heb 3:5). Moses was distinctive in his willingness for others to lead in his stead (e.g., Exod 4:13; 18:13–27; Num 11:29). Peter stressed this same emphasis when he spoke to the elders, as shepherds who are eager to serve (1 Pet 5:2). He reminded them not to lord it over those they are entrusted with (1 Pet 5:3), going on to direct all believers to be humble (1 Pet 5:5–6).

Like Moses and Jesus, all leaders should be examples of humility, just as all believers are expected to be humble. Normally, servants serve people who are richer or greater. In the Christian community, this is disrupted. There is no one-sided duty for people with less to serve those with more. Instead, the community's focus is on loving one another (John 15:9–17). Jesus repeatedly stressed the disciples' equality of status. Similarly, the leaders' role is to strengthen the community through promoting its members serving one another.

Often, the image of servant is distorted to justify individual community members' demands that leaders meet each of their personal needs. Insecure leaders who fail to understand their commitment to the whole community often burn themselves out. They lose their focus, trying to meet personally the various needs and dependencies of each individual in the community. The leader is not the only servant in Jesus's community. Jesus ordered the whole community of disciples to serve one another. Through our love for one another we, together, show the world that we are Jesus's disciples (John 13:35).

Leaders nurture multidirectional care within the community as both leaders and followers learn to love one another. Leaders, as servants of the whole community for Jesus's sake, focus on what is in the best interests of all believers together (2 Cor 4:5; 6:4; 1 Pet 5:2). Leaders' servant duty is to enable the whole community to serve their collective Lord by humbly caring for one another.

> LEADERS NURTURE MULTIDIRECTIONAL CARE WITHIN THE COMMUNITY.

Cultivate Generosity

God expects his household to grow and his resources to multiply. He wants life in all its fullness. Life makes itself obvious through reproduction. In the parable of the talents (Matt 25:14–30), the Master gives three servants resources to manage on their Master's behalf. When the Master calls his servants back, it is clear that he expected them to multiply his resources. It is sobering that the Master condemned the servant who simply maintained (stored) what he gave. God expects his people to grow his resources. This helps clarify how God wants us to use what he gives.

God gives power to leaders so they can multiply it in others. He gives resources so they can be multiplied for others. The biblical principle for multiplication is to give generously (Luke 6:38) and to sow the seeds of life (Matt 13:8).

Leaders manage God's household. Paul instructs both Titus and Timothy that one selection test for leaders is managing their own households well. As managers of God's household, leaders have to be blameless in character (Titus 1:7) and care for resources and people well (1 Tim 3:4–5). In contrast to the manager in the parable of the evil servant (Matt 24:45–51), the Master's resources are not for personal exploitation, nor his people for abuse.

Good management fosters joy. Leaders sometimes use Hebrews 13:17 like a spiritual bludgeon to try to force people to do what the leaders want. This is an inappropriate use of this verse. The author of Hebrews highlights that if leaders can do their work joyfully, this benefits the community. As we develop leaders, let's work on helping them to learn how to manage the resources entrusted to them in such a way that it brings them, and their community, joy.

Generous leaders genuinely want others to prosper. They make it easy for others to do the good works prepared in advance for them for the sake of the church and the wider community (Eph 2:10; 4:11–12). Anita Koeshall remarks,

> When God's Spirit transforms a person, power-striving instead becomes power-giving, a desire to increase the capacity and capabilities of others so that they can best accomplish their part in the mission of the community.[2]

Generosity is a quality of character which continuously promotes and supports the best in others.

What we receive, we receive to pass on to others. When Jesus sent out his twelve disciples on an extended ministry trip, he told them, "Give as freely as you have received" (Matt 10:8). This applies as equally to spiritual power as it does to material resources and knowledge. Jesus also warned us that the more we receive, more will be required from us (Luke 12:48). Jesus's standard for how the "more" should be used is carrying out his instructions. He expects his household to grow and prosper according to the values important to him.

LEADERS MANAGE GOD'S RESOURCES GENEROUSLY.

---
2 Koeshall, "Navigating Power."

Leaders are stewards not just of material resources but also of what they learn. Things that leaders learn through leadership development are not just for their personal development; they should be shared with the group. In the African Leadership Study, people surveyed said their leaders were influential because they remained connected to their communities. Even though they left those communities for a time to receive further training and education, they returned and shared what they learned with others.[3]

God has entrusted us all, together, with everything we need to make new disciples (e.g., Matt 7:7; 2 Tim 3:16–17; John 16:7–15). Neither the gospel nor disciples belong to leaders; they are God's (1 Cor 4:1–2; Titus 1:7). If we understand that God has made us responsible together, we cannot abrogate our responsibility solely to leaders. In our role as developers, we have to actively address any tendency in ourselves, leaders, or church members to assign ownership of the church, or its management responsibility, to leaders alone.

Leaders are stewards among stewards. God gives the resources of his household to the whole body of Christ to manage on his behalf. It is a subtle but significant distortion to apply parables about stewards (or managers) only to leaders, as if this is unique to leaders. We are all, together, given gifts, talents, and responsibility to multiply the Master's resources and work for the well-being and prosperity of his household. We may delegate to leaders some tasks of stewardship according to their gifting or position in the community. But, altogether, we will have to account for our management of what Jesus has given to us individually and corporately. In other words, the steward parables are not exclusive to leaders or a justification for setting them apart.

Leaders' relationship with their community, including how much they value it, is critical to Christian leadership. As shepherds, they nurture its fullness of life. As servants, they develop quality communal life through promoting one-another care. As stewards, leaders multiply resources, power, and life through freely giving on to others what they receive. However, because in their role they receive status and access to community resources, leaders are vulnerable to the corrupting influence of power and riches. In chapter 7 we examine these vulnerabilities that are a major challenge for all Christian leaders.

---

3 Ngaruiya, "Characteristics of Influential African Leaders," 1045, Kindle.

CHAPTER 7

GUARD AGAINST LEADERS' VULNERABILITIES

There are two areas of particular vulnerability for leaders: power and riches. It is easy for any of us who are leaders to forget that what we receive is not for our own benefit or because of our own intrinsic greatness. Power—the capacity to influence others—can corrupt us all. Having influence can cause us to want to use it for our own benefit. Sometimes our purpose seems good. But if it is not God's purpose, and does not nurture and multiply the community of disciples, we have corrupted the power entrusted to us.

In the same way, riches tend to corrupt us. When we receive material resources for the community, sometimes we think that because we have access to them they are ours to use as we like. It can be very difficult not to help ourselves to some of these resources. We justify this by thinking that we have earned or deserve them. We tell ourselves that the way we would like to use them is the best way.

It is difficult to separate vulnerability to power from vulnerability to riches, because having access to riches increases leaders' ability to influence. By controlling access to resources, leaders can cause people to do what they—the leaders—want.

Power easily corrupts, and Christian leaders are not immune to its corrupting influence. Evangelicals have been documenting this problem since at least the 1980s, when Ted Ward wrote "Servants, Leaders, and Tyrants."[1]

Jane Overstreet has spent over two decades working with Christian leaders from around the world. She concludes that the most prominent stumbling block to healthy churches and Christian organizations is power-hoarding leadership. She labels this "big boss leadership." Big boss leaders tell those they lead, "Since I have the leadership, I can do whatever I want

---

1 Ward, "Servants, Leaders, and Tyrants."

to do, and you have to do whatever I say because you are under me." Overstreet sees this as "an ugly perversion of what God intends leaders to be."[2] Such leaders damage the health of churches. They limit growth because the leaders themselves become the focus, rather than the community.

In the Bible we find some notable examples of otherwise good leaders misusing power. Moses and Aaron abused God's power when Moses struck the rock to draw out water for the Israelite community (Num 20:1–13). Moses was frustrated with the people. Rather than simply speaking to the rock in God's name, Moses shouted, "Listen, you rebels! Must we bring you water from this rock?" God condemned them for this because it showed lack of trust in God. It gave the people the false impression that the power came from them rather than God. David, although being a man after God's own heart (1 Sam 13:14), abused his power by taking another man's wife and having him killed (2 Sam 11).

Three key temptations for every Christian leader are similar to Jesus's temptations in the wilderness (Matt 4:1–11). The first temptation, for Jesus to turn stones into bread to satisfy his hunger, is the temptation to use God-given power wrongfully for personal desires. The second temptation for leaders—parallel to Satan tempting Jesus to jump off the Temple and trust that God's angels would catch and protect him—is to become spectacular and wonderful in people's eyes. This corrupts leaders' opinion of themselves so they believe they are greater than others, rather than staying close to followers and revealing their personal weaknesses. The third temptation—like Satan tempting Jesus to bow down to him so that he could rule all the kingdoms of the world—is the temptation to use power to rule over others. This includes controlling, manipulating, or exploiting them according to what we want, rather than loving them in humility.[3]

Power corrupts because gaining it makes us want more. It makes us forget that we are accountable. Power-abusing leaders deliberately manipulate people to get them to do what leaders want. These leaders are controllers. They are power-seeking or power-hoarding rather than power-giving.[4] They use their position and authority to ensure the results they want, including getting more power for themselves. Sometimes they do this unwittingly. They act on the false belief that only they know what is best for the group. They think their way is the only way.

---

2 Overstreet, *Unleader*, 10.
3 The ideas in this paragraph are drawn from Henri Nouwen, *In the Name of Jesus*.
4 The term "power-seeking leaders" is described and contrasted with "power-giving leaders" in Lingenfelter, *Leading Cross-Culturally*, 105–19.

When leaders abuse power, they invert their role as shepherd-protectors of the flock and become a danger to it. Power is given to us to protect and nurture life in all its fullness. If we exert it for our own benefit, then we exploit, manipulate, or control others; and in doing so, we harm them. Abuse of power affects all four critical characteristics of leadership. Leaders setting themselves apart from followers disrupts the community. Leaders' personal agendas subvert the clarity that should help transform the community for God's purposes. Leaders become negative examples, displaying what disciples should *not* be.

Instead of being servants of the community, power-abusing leaders serve themselves. The balance of relationships becomes unequal. Disciples focus on serving the leader instead of caring for and building up one another. By hoarding power for their own benefit, leaders divert followers' service away from God and one another, toward the leader.

If leaders misuse community resources, they do the opposite of what they should do as stewards. When leaders use community resources for themselves, this harms the leaders' character. It fosters a love of money. The community also does not receive what it needs. This often causes conflict in the community because of lack of resources. It disrupts members' ability to care for one another. Their arguing turns their attention away from the community's purpose.

Extreme power-hoarders are tyrant leaders. They exclude others from any involvement in decision-making and ministry. In a church in Europe that we were part of, the pastor suddenly made a one-sided decision to merge three churches into one big church. The pastor gave congregation members no opportunity to discuss this decision. Some people felt that this would hinder evangelism, discipling, and the overall growth of the church. A couple of congregation members challenged the pastor. They asked him who he was accountable to. The pastor replied, "I am like Moses. I have been given this vision by God and I only need to answer to him."

> HELP LEADERS TO EMPOWER OTHERS AND INTENTIONALLY SEEK ACCOUNTABILITY.

This same kind of one-man-band, power-hoarding leadership caused many Millet Christians in Bulgaria to leave their churches. These leaders believed they were doing God's will and caring for the needs of their churches. In reality, though, their way of leading destroyed relationships and harmed the spiritual and emotional health of many churches.[5]

---
5 Richard Hibbert, "Why Do They Leave?"

Leaders who intentionally seek accountability from their followers, and who empower and publicly value their followers, are more able to avoid the corrupting effect of power. This is because they effectively use external means to safeguard their internal principles. The American evangelist, Billy Graham, is a good example of a leader who intentionally guarded his and other ministry members' integrity. He did this early in his ministry through setting up accountability external to himself. With his founding team, he agreed on practices to guard their financial and moral integrity. These became integral to his personal and organizational practice.[6] Keeping to these practices and allowing people around him to reinforce them, ensured transparency about finances and protection from sexual temptation and false accusations.

The community protects leaders from power by setting up accountability structures. Large power-distance cultures usually have very well-defined structures. The same hierarchies exist in most organizations. The role of leaders and surrounding people is clear to everyone. For example, an older senior pastor in many Korean or Chinese churches will be supported by a group of mature peers as elders. These elders act both as advisers to the senior leader and as mediators between the senior leader and the congregation.

HELP THE COMMUNITY SET UP TRANSPARENT ACCOUNTABILITY STRUCTURES.

Although outsiders mainly notice the senior leader, the elders are continuously at work in the background. In these cases, the people are the accountability structure. Relationships between the leader and supporters are key to effective accountability.

In small power-distance cultures, the accountability structures and leader's role are often set up during the leader's appointment. They change from organization to organization. A common example of this is written job descriptions, including lines of accountability. Accountability often happens through committees reviewing written reports. The aim is to separate accountability from relationships. Accountability is ensured through written reports and evaluations according to performance based on written requirements. In small power distance contexts, this decreased reliance on relational factors is considered to protect against the corruption that can occur through people exploiting relationships for personal gain.

Accountability means followers give leaders power but structurally constrain how they use it. The constraints may be a hierarchy of people or a procedure of reports and review by committees. Either way, members of the community check what leaders are doing. When these structural

---

6 E.g., https://billygraham.org/story/the-modesto-manifesto-a-declaration-of-biblical-integrity/.

constraints weaken or fail, leaders may wield their power like a tyrant, since followers do not have the means to address the misuse of power.

In small power-distance cultures, it may be more difficult for leaders to gain significant power, as power is more equally shared. In small power-distance situations, leaders seeking to get power are prone to manipulating, politicking, and competing for control.[7] Leaders' wielding of their power in low power-distance contexts may not be as obvious, but it is just as open to abuse as in large power-distance contexts. In either situation, "abuse of power" means leaders are ignoring or deliberately undermining checks and balances that the community would normally set in place.

All cultures have structures to limit the use of power. They also have ways of managing resources to ensure accountability to the community. Human weakness regarding riches is recognized in all cultures. Accountability protects leaders and communities. Abuse of power is such a big problem that societies have ways of protecting communities as well. These include review of records by outsiders, governance boards, and externally appointed outside overseers. Journalism is another form of accountability. Journalists are expert investigators and exposers of secret corruption. Prophets and whistleblowers also force leaders to be accountable. They fearlessly speak out publicly to raise awareness of corruption. Fear of exposure can help leaders to be careful about what they do.

Transparency builds community trust. The more people who know what is going on, the less leaders can pursue personal agendas at the expense of the community. In many contexts, the community makes sure that leaders don't personally manage material resources. When everyone knows what is happening and leaders don't personally handle community resources, the community feels secure.

The temptation to mishandle material resources is easier to protect against than abuse of power. Power is subjective. It can be difficult to explain what exactly is happening. Those experiencing abuse are not confident about how they interpret it. Protection normally happens by surrounding leaders with a group of people. These people protect leaders through their relationship with them, their presence in potentially corrupting situations, and through their observation of leaders as they lead. They advise and are empowered to intervene when necessary. They can help leaders reflect on their actions, motivations, and the effect of their influence over others.

In gross abuse of power leading to sexual immorality or other exploitation of followers, where outsiders have the power to do so they

---

7 Koeshall, "Navigating Power," 67.

will step in to remove the corrupt leaders. This has occurred recently with secular journalists and governments intervening to address child sexual abuse in Christian institutions in the Western world. Sadly, abuse of power may continue for a long time before outsiders are willing to intervene. Because followers are a reflection of their leaders, churches may resist their leaders' exposure, even when they are aware of the leaders' failings.

So far, we have discussed where leaders knowingly abuse power and riches. Sadly, leaders' unconscious bias can cause them to exploit or harm some members of the community. Most commonly this occurs in relation to gender, ethnic minorities, and disabilities. This is systemic injustice. The system is a society-wide problem. Leaders who come from a dominant group in society act in a biased way toward minority-group members. They are unaware of problems in their attitudes.

A common example of this is to exclude people with minority ethnic backgrounds from leadership in churches and Christian institutions. This is often justified by claiming that a lack of qualified people are available. They do not realize that "qualified" means people who are like them. This bias affects not only the selection but also the mentoring and support that minority-group leaders receive. Leaders committed to seeing their whole community flourish will be more ready to address this unconscious abuse of power that devalues some members of the community.

Research Vulnerabilities and Accountability

> ENABLE LEADERS TO IDENTIFY RED-FLAG FEELINGS AND KNOW HOW TO CHANGE.

Our role as developers is to foster culturally fitting accountability. To do this well, we not only need to understand these vulnerabilities generally, we need to research them specifically in the leaders' cultural context. We should learn how leaders gain power and how they use it. We can look into how they influence people, what that power feels like for leaders when they wield it, and how those who experience its abuse feel. Feelings are important. We can often recognize them before we can explain what is happening. These feelings act like red flags to help leaders and followers identify when change is needed. This could be in leaders themselves or the support structures around them.

Different cultures express the principles of transparency and accountability differently. Transparency is defined by who is watching and how much it is reasonable for them to see. For example, transparency in weak group-orientation cultures rarely extends beyond the front door of the home. People in low context-orientation cultures value written reports more than what leaders or others say. In strongly group-oriented, high-context cultures, leaders' whole lives will be on display. These are discussed throughout the community. Community members give value to what leaders say, but the "saying" will include far more than the words spoken. In small power-distance cultures, people may confront leaders directly. In large power-distance cultures, especially those in which honor and face are valued, leaders will usually be challenged indirectly, often using skilled, trusted mediators.

We should research the types of benefits leaders in the culture normally receive. We can learn how people in the local culture believe these benefits should be used, and how they hold their leaders accountable for their use. That is, we should be clear about local people's expectations about leaders' stewardship of community resources.

It is also important to learn how people in the local culture try to protect leaders and their communities from abuse of power. As developers, we should affirm both local (intracommunity) measures as well as wider society's approaches. Our focus should be on strengthening local ways of doing things rather than trying to impose our own culture's practices.

To help leaders deal with unconscious bias against some members of the community, we, with leaders, should also explore bias and power imbalances between groups in the local context. This can help us understand dynamics between leaders and members of the groups they lead, as well as dynamics between group members.

Model Self-Awareness

As developers, we need to admit our own vulnerability to power and riches. We can then develop leaders' and their communities' awareness of these vulnerabilities. We should affirm and strengthen culturally fitting ways of ensuring transparency and accountability. We can help leaders learn to reflect on themselves—their actions, attitudes, and biases. And we can help communities protect their leaders, and themselves, against corruption from power and riches.

The best way to learn self-awareness and recognition of when we are manipulating others is through mentoring. We learn from feedback from observers in real life or simulated experiences. The aim is to develop self-reflection. We can model how to apologize and ask for forgiveness for attitudes and behaviors associated with these vulnerable areas. We can be an example of how to self-correct quickly when we are tempted to relapse.

When mentoring or modeling more difficult character areas like these, it is important to make our thoughts explicit. This means stating out loud what is going on inside us. This can help leaders develop healthy self-reflective and self-corrective thinking habits. Specific training in valuing and empowering others may also help.

Leadership-training programs or books on Christian leadership rarely address abuse of power. Yet it is one of the first things the secular world is quick to recognize as wrong in Christian leaders. Christian leadership should be exemplary in this area. History, sadly, tells another story.

Because communities give their leaders power and riches, leaders are particularly vulnerable to corruption. In chapter 8 we explore the relationship between leaders and communities in more depth.

Chapter 8

Strengthen the Community (C1)

The Bible consistently highlights the community of God's people. It is as we love one another that we show the world that we are Jesus's disciples (John 13:35). It is as a whole group that we receive gifts to build up the body of Christ (Eph 4:11–16). Throughout the Bible, God is continually calling out a people for himself who can join in community with him (1 Pet 2:9–10). Leaders are integral to this community. Together with followers, they are responsible for building it up as a whole.

Most *you's* in the Bible are plural. More than two thousand of the three thousand *you's* in the New Testament refer to "you-all." Most of these refer to the community of God's people.[1] Those of us brought up in weak group-oriented cultures interpret what we read in Scripture through an individualistic lens. English increases this bias because it does not distinguish between the singular and plural *you*. Even when the context implies a plural *you*, individualistic bias causes the reader to interpret the *you* as singular, or individual.

The primary question we should ask of any Bible passage is "What is it saying to us, together, as a church, family, or wider community," rather than "What does this passage mean for me?" As developers, our role is to help leaders strengthen the togetherness inherent in being God's people.

Leaders are an integral part of the groups they lead. The capacity of people to lead a group depends on the group not only identifying those people as leaders but also faithfully supporting them. Douglas McConnell says, "Leaders learn to lead in communities that learn to follow. The two are inseparable."[2]

---

[1] The Pioneers' New Testament, Word Study #142: "You, You-all, and Each of You," https://pioneernt.com/2012/04/25/word-study-142-you-you-all-and-each-of-you/.

[2] McConnell, *Cultural Insights for Christian Leaders*, 515, Kindle.

Individualism strongly affects Westerners' assumptions about leadership and its development. Most Westerners tend to see leadership as solo. Most books on leadership are written from this perspective. As developers, we have to be careful not to separate leaders from the groups they lead.

God has given the church all kinds of gifts. The gift of leadership is just one of them. The multiplicity of gifts creates an interdependence that strengthens the community. God intends these gifts and roles to work together to grow his community (Rom 12:1–8; 1 Cor 12:12–31; Eph 4:11–16). In God's eyes, *all* the gifts are essential for the healthy functioning of Christ's body.

If the leader separates out as a super-individual, it hinders the leader, the church, and the wider community from flourishing. This super-role is impossible for a lone individual to carry out successfully. Sadly, but not surprisingly, it often results in failure and burnout. We need one another. All—leaders and non-leaders—have a role to play in helping the whole community of believers grow in Christ.

Keep Leaders in Their Communities

The New Testament explains that leaders are fellow siblings with other believers. Leaders and followers are all priests who have the same Master, Teacher, and Father in heaven (Matt 12:46–50; 1 Pet 2:9). Jesus taught that even the apostles—the leaders with the greatest authority in the early church—were to be "among" rather than lording their authority over their siblings in Christ (Matt 23:5–12).

Leadership is a two-way relationship. Followers influence leaders, and leaders influence followers. Followers continually evaluate their leaders' ways of leading. They react either positively or negatively depending on whether the leaders meet their expectations and fit their picture of good leadership. If they appreciate the way leaders are leading, they will affirm and reinforce the leaders' behavior. Leaders then continue thinking and behaving in the same way. A good fit between leaders and followers occurs. Leaders' leadership is effective as followers accept it.

> STRENGTHEN THE TWO-WAY RELATIONSHIP BETWEEN LEADERS AND FOLLOWERS.

On the other hand, if followers judge their leaders' way of leading negatively, they will react negatively. The leaders will then, hopefully, revise their way of leading. If they don't, followers are likely to withdraw their loyalty and, therefore, their followership. Even if leaders keep an official role, followers will ignore or subvert their leadership.

Leaders and followers are naturally more interconnected in strong versus weak group-oriented cultures. In sub-Saharan African *ubuntu*, each person is expected to contribute to the whole community as well as to create and nurture ties of friendship through which benefit can flow.[3] Leaders are integral to this network of relationships, not separate from or above it.

In Korea, the leader is inseparable from the group and stands for it. As related in Korean television dramas, for example, when even the most junior member of a group makes a mistake, it affects the whole group's standing (or honor) in society. It is not uncommon for the leader, who has done nothing wrong, to resign because of the group's failing. In contrast, in Anglo-American dramas, individual leaders protect their standing by scapegoating more junior individuals, even when it is the leader's mistake.

Evalde Mutabazi explained how a Congolese founder of a cheese-making company built on the African idea of *ubuntu* in order to enable his workers to become a community that worked together to produce high-quality cheese. Foremen in charge of each cheese-making area met weekly to share with one another about their part of the process. This meant that the foreman in charge of collecting milk became aware of the problems faced by his colleagues in manufacturing and selling cheese and vice versa. The foremen also organized work meetings with their own teams to share the issues, problems, and what they were learning week by week. This emphasis on healthy relationships forged a common commitment to working together between leaders and everyone else in the company.[4]

In contrast to leaders being among their sisters and brothers, the stereotypical lone male Christian leader is set apart from his church and community. One of the most frequent complaints we heard from Millet believers about pastors was "He has set himself apart from us. He looks down on us as if he is better than us."

David Bennett comments that lifting and isolating leaders puts them "on a hierarchical ladder where they ascend further and further from identification with ordinary believers."[5] This is in direct opposition to God's design for Christian community.

Kevin Hovey, a missionary to Papua New Guinea for three decades, was appointed by the executive leadership of the national church he worked with to be a consultant for them. Among the issues this leadership group

---

3 Mutabazi, "Preparing African Leaders," 214.
4 Mutabazi, 215–18.
5 Bennett, "The Leader as ... Friend ... Brother/Sister ... Servant ... ," 15.

wrestled with was what to do about Australian pastors who were flying into PNG to give one- to two-week Bible-teaching seminars. One of the PNG leaders explained:

> We love the teaching these pastors bring. They have knowledge of the Bible that we don't have. ... But every time they come, no matter which one it is, they sow in seeds of arrogance, independence, and discord into our movement, which has such a thriving sense of unanimity that we thank God for. Should we write a letter and implement a moratorium on their coming?

These leaders were deeply concerned because they were hearing the Australian pastors teach a view of leadership that stated, "You are leader. If you are a God-called leader, you have to lead and make decisions [on your own]."

The Australian pastors were unconsciously promoting solo, independent, arrogant leadership. In contrast, the PNG leaders valued leaders working with other leaders for the well-being of the whole group.

Separating leaders from their communities for training can result in several negative consequences. Leaders can feel as if they are members of an elite. Elite people are judged by different standards than others. Church members feel they can't challenge leaders' immature or inappropriate behavior. They can't hold leaders accountable. Then the only people who can hold the leaders accountable become the missionaries or other outsiders who appointed them. Finally, without community accountability, these leaders become more vulnerable to temptation.

David's sin with Bathsheba was preceded by his not being with his soldiers in battle, as he was expected to be (2 Sam 11:1). God condemned the rich people in Israel because they separated themselves from the rest of the people. He rebuked them because their increased property had isolated them from the rest of the community, causing them to be "alone in the land" (Isa 5:8).

In Bulgaria, missionaries or Bulgarian pastors often singled out Millet men to be pastors. Church members were usually not consulted and had no recourse to challenge the appointment. This way of selecting leaders ignored standards the Millet already had for recognizing leaders.

Richard interviewed Millet church members, as well as church and community leaders. He found that the first quality they look for in a leader is the ability to uphold the welfare and honor of the group (whether church or extended family). They show care and respect for group members by patiently listening to each member and respecting the overall "feeling" of the group. For the Millet, leaders are people with life experience. They have wisdom, trustworthiness, and a good reputation inside and outside the group.[6] When these standards were ignored by missionaries or Bulgarians, relationships between appointed leaders and their churches, and the wider Millet neighborhood, became strained.

Many newly appointed Millet leaders received a large influx of material resources. These were mainly clothing, food, and money, provided by other (foreign or Bulgarian) churches and Christian organizations. Donors gave these resources to leaders to give out to their churches and communities. Church members and others in the Millet community became suspicious about the way leaders were doling out these resources. Many suspected that leaders were favoring their own families. Some church members felt hurt and overlooked, leading some to leave the church.[7] It didn't matter what the leaders actually did. Leaders' separation from their communities created distrust. It meant there was no community-based transparency or accountability.

The experience of some Mursi (a seminomadic tribe in Ethiopia) younger people shows the negative consequences of separating people from their community for learning. A missionary who lived among the Mursi for more than a decade related to us what happened. Some Mursi youth left home to be educated in the city. This was for general education, not leadership development. When they returned to Mursi-land, they brought with them a new view of how to do things in the community and church. The young men's education apart from their community and its context caused them to disrespect the older leaders in both the community and the church.

A conflict arose between the youths' view and that of the traditional leaders. The traditional leaders were older men with a reputation for wisdom and Christian maturity. The older men saw the youths as uncommitted. The youths considered the older men as being "back in the Dark Ages, or perhaps even unbiblical compared to what they had seen in the outside world." There were, no doubt, some advantages of outside education for the youths, and potentially for the tribe. But it also created spiritual danger for the youths. They viewed themselves as an elite, better than the older leaders, because they had gained special knowledge not available to the rest of the believers.

---

6 Hibbert and Hibbert, "Defining Culturally Appropriate Leadership."
7 Hibbert, "Why Do They Leave?"

Ubuntu reinforces that leadership development should value the leaders' networks of relationships. We should help leaders nurture healthy relationships with their families, friends, and fellow believers, as well as people in the broader community. Weak group-oriented developers should cultivate the discipline of looking beyond individual leaders to the web of people connected to the leaders. This can have a practical impact on planned leadership-development programs. Sometimes leaders' relationships have a higher priority than planned activities.

VALUE THE LEADERS' NETWORKS OF RELATIONSHIPS.

An example of this, as reported by an Australian missionary serving in Tanzania, was leaders leaving a training program for significant periods every time a relative—even a distant relative—died. These Tanzanian leaders needed to pay their respects to and support the family of the deceased. Developers need to value these relational webs and be flexible enough to work with them. This is in contrast to seeing them as obstructing learning.

Look for Community Endorsement

For leaders to lead, the community they belong to must endorse them. The community has to show publicly their willingness to follow. During the time the Hebrews were slaves in Egypt, Pharaoh ruled over them. But the Hebrews did not recognize him as their leader. He was not part of their community, nor did he want to be. He used his power to compel the Israelites to work for the benefit of Pharaoh's own people. Even Moses was not automatically accepted as their leader. It took time for him to win the Israelites' approval. It required God's backing of him displayed through miracles to convince them to accept him as their leader. It is worth noting that their commitment was fickle, in the sense that they periodically rebelled against his leadership. He had to keep winning back their endorsement.

God gives gifts of leadership to some people for the benefit of the community. We can expect Christian communities to recognize these gifts and other qualities of good leaders. Louis Ao and David Penley write:

> Leaders must be confirmed. A leader cannot simply proclaim himself a leader. Others must confirm that they see God's hand at work in his life, that he exemplifies the characteristics of biblical leadership, and that he is a mature and growing person who has the skills to lead others to do likewise.[8]

---
8 Ao and Penley, *Cross-Cultural Leadership*, 155.

Throughout Scripture, leaders are recognized by the communities they go on to lead. God instructed Moses, for example, to appoint leaders who had a good reputation in the community (Deut 1:12–13). John the Baptist, Jesus's first disciples, and religious leaders such as Nicodemus all affirmed Jesus's leadership (John 1:29–51; 3:2). Barnabas was recognized as being "a good man, full of the Holy Spirit and strong in faith" and for this reason the church at Jerusalem sent him to Antioch as their representative (Acts 11:24).

Paul told Timothy and Titus to appoint, as elders in the church, individuals

- whose lives could not be spoken against (1 Tim 3:2)
- who were well thought of for their good life (Titus 1:6)
- who had a good reputation—both inside the church and in the surrounding community (1 Tim 3:2)

Often, outsiders choose leaders who their communities do not endorse. For example, they choose young men who can speak the missionaries' language or the dominant language well (e.g., the German language in a multicultural church in Germany or the Bulgarian language in Bulgaria). Missionaries choose people who have had more formal schooling or unemployed young men, because they are more available. Sometimes people who attend a dominant-culture church are chosen (e.g., a Bulgarian church in Bulgaria).

Usually there is minimal or no consultation with members of the community. Group members then defer responsibility and accountability for the new leaders to the outsiders who appointed them. Too often this results in leaders who are plagued by lack of community support, moral failure, and financial problems. The community becomes disillusioned. We could avoid many of these problems by seeking their community's endorsement before appointing leaders.

Communities will not endorse leaders if they cannot relate to the people within the community. They need to be able to build healthy, trusting relationships with people in their own community. We can assess their relationship-building capacity through relatively simple ministry. Their leading or coleading a small group, such as a Bible-study group or community-outreach group, for a few months is a good way of doing this. At the end of this time, if the group does not trust the leader, that person is not yet ready to continue leading this or any other group.

Strengthen Community Decision-Making Processes

A major role of leadership is helping the community decide what it should do and how to use its resources. How much leaders involve the community in decision-making varies from culture to culture. Highly "participative" leaders encourage all community members to join in discussion about what to do. Highly "autocratic" leaders do not consult members. Different cultures lie between these two extremes.

Participative leaders believe that involving followers in discussion and debate is a natural part of good decision-making.[9] Countries characterized by small power distance, low uncertainty avoidance, and weak group orientation prize participative leadership. North Americans, Canadians, Australians, New Zealanders, Scandinavians, and people from the UK expect their leaders to involve them in decision-making.[10]

Participation in decision-making is expressed in various ways in different cultures. In weak group-oriented cultures, meetings where everyone can speak to the whole group are the norm. In Austria, people expect leaders not only to listen to their ideas but to include them in the final decisions. In the US, people care about whether the leader treats them as equals. Although they expect leaders to listen to their ideas, they don't necessarily expect them to include their ideas in final decisions.[11]

People from some cultures—especially more group-oriented cultures with large power distance and high uncertainty avoidance—have less expectation that leaders will involve them in decision-making. Or leaders do it in less obvious ways. Most of the countries of Latin Europe, Latin America, Eastern Europe, the Middle East, Confucian Asia, Southern Asia, and sub-Saharan Africa fall into this category. They trust their leaders to make decisions that are in the best interests of the community and are comfortable with leaders who act more like fathers than like brothers.

Nevertheless, research in some of these countries has found that people still want some participation. In Greece and Mexico, for example, people want to be invited to share their opinions and have their suggestions listened to. However, they don't expect to have much direct influence on decision-making.[12]

In some strongly group-oriented cultures, the leader gathers individual views outside the meeting of the whole group. People can express their

---

9 House, *Strategic Leadership across Cultures*, 69.
10 Brodbeck, Chhokar, and House, "Culture and Leadership in 25 Societies," 1040.
11 Brodbeck, Chhokar, and House, 1041.
12 Brodbeck, Chhokar, and House, 72.

views in these one-on-one or small-group meetings without fearing the reactions of more powerful voices in the wider group. In this approach, neither leader nor follower loses face if the person expresses a view with which no one else agrees.

> FOSTER HEALTHY, CULTURALLY FITTING, GROUP DECISION-MAKING.

This is in evidence in the Japanese *ringi* system of decision-making. In this system, leaders develop consensus through individual discussions before they make a final decision.[13] Deciding takes longer, but it results in much more robust decisions. Group members know their voice has been heard and trust the leaders to weigh up carefully everyone's contributions.

Both autocratic leadership and participative leadership have flaws. Autocratic leaders can create fear and distrust. They sometimes ignore information from followers and rely on their own judgment alone.[14] But participative leadership is not always positive. Participative leaders can default to allowing the loudest or most powerful individuals to have the most influential voices. Sometimes the participative process results in paralysis. The leaders cannot find consensus between the multiple agendas in the group.

As developers, we should invest time watching and learning how groups in the leaders' context make decisions. We should mentor and support leaders in healthy, culturally fitting, group decision-making. A sign of health is when the community enjoys working together, with each member feeling valued by the leaders.

Include the Community in Leaders' Development

People develop people. Developers are not the only people forming leaders. A recent multicountry study of African Christian leaders found that Christian leaders who are influential in their communities had been formed by their communities. These leaders explained that their growth as leaders involved a series of incremental steps. The first step was nurture within their family and circle of friends. It was built on by the relationships they formed in educational institutions. Existing leaders developed them further through accepting them as apprentices, mentoring them, and giving them responsibilities. Their growth into leadership was not a one-time activity. There were many "incremental investments" from other people along the way.[15]

---

13 Matsumoto, *Culture and Psychology*.
14 Bass and Bass, *Bass Handbook of Leadership*, 440.
15 Gitau, "Formation of African Christian Leaders," 1599–644.

We teach as we have been taught. Many developers have been trained according to an individualistic pattern focusing on each leader's personal development. It can be difficult to envisage ways of training that include the community and have its well-being as a vital aim. To overcome this individualistic pattern, we can do four things. We can arrange for mentoring or teaching by more mature or skilled members of the community. We can ask community members to give feedback on the leaders' development. We can make sure that whatever leaders learn, they apply in their communities. We can teach in such a way that leaders can pass on what they learn to the rest of their community. Evaluation of leadership development should include how well the community is developing, as well as its leaders.

It is good to open training events to other Christians beyond leaders. This will offset any impression in the community that secret knowledge is being made available only to a privileged elite. It is likely that most will not be able or want to come, but a few may. They should be made to feel welcome.

A missionary working in Tanzania experienced this. A local bishop asked him to help train pastors, evangelists, and other lay leaders in several villages. The training sessions occurred under the shade of a tree. About twenty other people, apart from the leaders, would always join them. These others wanted to listen and learn what they could. The older people among them were given the more honorable seats at the front. It was important for everyone to be included because they all felt part of the group.

Beyond feeling included, community members can also remind leaders of what they have learned. They can strengthen leaders' understanding by asking them to explain further. They can also hold leaders accountable for putting into practice what they have learned.

Ideally, we should include the local Christian community when planning leaders' development. They are the people who best understand the local situation. They can give input into the kinds of leaders the community is looking for. They will know where gaps in leaders' abilities and qualities are. They will have opinions about the best outcomes for leaders and the community. If we invite them to join in leadership-development events, they will be able to provide insights on how any theory applies to their context. They will also be able to give feedback on how suitable and effective it is.

> EVALUATE COMMUNITIES, NOT JUST LEADERS.

Existing local Christian leaders will be the best people to deliver training and to evaluate trainees. Giving the community a voice in leadership development means including as many members of the community as possible, not just leaders. After all, all community members have a vested interest in the development of leaders.

Promote Community Values through Group-Based Learning

Because of the importance of community for leaders, we should plan for leaders to be developed in groups or in the local community. This is already important for learning in strongly group-oriented cultures. A German technician was attempting to train Japanese people to use a machine. The German technician's training approach was to single out Japanese trainees and train them one by one. After a while, the Japanese manager approached him and said, "I am sorry, we are a group and we expect to be trained together. Please, could you show us, as a group, how to use the machine?"[16]

It was obvious to the Japanese participants that training to use the machine would work better for them if done as a group. But someone who is weakly group-oriented—in this case the German technician—is not likely to see this without some prompting.

Leaders (and developers) with weak group orientation often need a lot of help to work out how to value the community in a practical way. If we make group orientation a value of our leadership development, this will help to make it a focus. Communicating this value as developers means to live it, not just say it.

The capacity of leaders to relate well to their communities is largely determined by their character. In chapter 9 we examine biblical expectations of leaders' character, and what the best ways to develop these are.

---

16 Elashmawi and Harris, *Multicultural Management*, 38.

CHAPTER 9

BUILD CHARACTER (C2)

A leader's character is the essence of who the leader is. Everything a leader says and does flows from this source (Matt 7:15–18; Mark 7:21). Leaders cannot create this essence by themselves. It is the result of God's work in their lives. It is the fruit of God's Spirit, who has been at work in the leaders over months or years: "The Lord—who is the Spirit—makes us more and more like him as we are changed into his glorious image" (2 Cor 3:18).

Godly character is the product of inner transformation, or the "renovation of the heart," to use Dallas Willard's phrase, that God has been effecting in leaders.[1] Leaders' lives are on display to both Christians and the wider community. This means the whole of leaders' lives is important, not just how they behave when they are with fellow Christians (1 Tim 3:2, 7; Titus 1:6–8; 1 Pet 5:3).

Since the source of godly character is God, good character depends on the leader's relationship with God. Just as is the case for all Jesus's followers, the fruit Christian leaders bear, in terms of godly character qualities, is the overflow of their fellowship with Jesus (John 15:1–8). Like the Apostle Paul, leaders need to know Christ more than anything else. They need to be able to say "everything else is worthless when compared with the infinite value of knowing Christ Jesus my Lord" (Phil 3:8, cf. Phil 3:8–10; 1:9–11; Eph 1:17; 3:16–19; Col 1:9–10).

More than a thousand Christian leaders from seven continents were asked how they define Christ-centered leadership. They repeatedly highlighted four qualities: integrity, authenticity, servant-heartedness, and humility.[2] Every one of these qualities is a matter of character rather than competency.

Another recent study found that Christian leaders across India believe that Indian churches most need leaders with Christlike character and

---
1 Willard, *Renovation of the Heart*.
2 Overstreet, *Unleader*, 9.

servant hearts.[3] African Christian-leadership research similarly concludes that Africa will only be transformed if "principled" and "ethical" leaders emerge.[4]

Gaining these qualities is not a static, one-time achievement. Leaders need to keep growing in them. That is why Peter writes, "The more you grow like this, the more productive and useful you will be in your knowledge of our Lord Jesus Christ" (2 Pet 1:8).

A person's character is fundamental to being a good leader because followers take on the character of their leaders. This is a natural result of leadership. It is also something that Paul encourages when he says, "I urge you to imitate me" (1 Cor 4:16; cf. 11:1; Phil 4:9). Leaders reproduce their core qualities in the groups they lead. Over time, the group begins to take on the character of the leader. This is partly why different churches and Christian organizations have different emphases, different subcultures, and different "flavors." In fact, if we want to understand leaders we should spend time closely watching the groups they are leading. The groups reflect their leaders and are their leaders' "exam paper."

Pain-bearing, resilience, courage, and integrity are especially important for leaders. This is because of the specific challenges that leaders face. Leaders become the focal point for communities and manage the community's problems. They deal with issues between members of the community, or at the boundary between the community and surrounding society. All disciples develop in these areas, but they should be a focus of leadership development.

Strengthen Capacity for Pain-Bearing

Christian leaders cannot avoid suffering that is extra to what most believers experience. Leaders should expect to suffer and willingly endure it when it comes (1 Pet 2:21). Jesus impressed on his disciples that they would suffer. He said they would need to be single-minded about enduring it for his sake (Mark 8:34–38; Luke 9:57–62; John 15:18).

Leadership brings pain into leaders' lives beyond the pain caused by their own personal difficulties. Leaders have to bear their own pain as well as the pain of those they lead. To lead well, leaders must be willing and able to carry this extra pain. Gary Corwin explains that however much leaders can bear the pain of others determines their capacity to lead.

---

3 David, "India Leadership Study."
4 Gitau, "Formation of African Christian Leaders," 1613, Kindle.

You can only exercise and sustain personal leadership to the extent that you can bear pain. If you can only bear your own pain, you can't really lead. If you can bear and respond only to the pain of your family, your family represents the full scope of your leadership potential. If, however, by God's grace you can recognize and bear the pain of those around you, the breadth of your leadership potential is limited only by the scope of your burden and capacity.[5]

Tokunbeh Adeyemo, formerly General Secretary of the Association for Evangelicals in Africa, includes leaders' hard work on behalf of others as pain-bearing, especially when nobody is aware of that hard work.

> Show me a church or state or community servant leader and I will prove to you a man or woman who practices self-denial, cross-bearing and discipline. A servant leader works long, late and hard while others are sleeping. He prays when others are playing. He studies the ruins and works out strategies while others are picnicking. A servant leader fasts while others feast. He constructs while others only have time to criticize.[6]

It is difficult to work hard and not be acknowledged. It is more difficult to work hard and then be criticized. Adeyemo's comment also raises the pain caused because leaders cannot do everything, nor should they. This is a recipe for burnout. We are limited human beings. It is painful to have to let go of all the things that could be done for the sake of what is humanly possible.

Leaders are pain-bearers because they become the focal point for the community. Insiders and outsiders blame leaders for community members' problems or what they think the community stands for.

Leaders need to develop the capacity to absorb pain rather than passing it on. Negativity communicated to leaders should stop at the leader. Leaders are gatekeepers. It is like absorbing poison rather than letting it spread. But leaders need to deal healthily with that poison rather than letting it cause harm to them personally. The gatekeeper's role is to open the gate to Jesus only and keep out what destroys.

> HELP LEADERS LEARN TO "CATCH" HARMFUL THINGS AND PASS THEM ON TO JESUS.

Leaders need to develop the capacity to divert things that harm by "catching" them and passing them on to Jesus to deal with. We do this by listening to grievances, admitting fault, and apologizing personally or on behalf of the community or its individual members. Then the leader must forgive and forget, or deal with problems without becoming an accuser. Instead of

---

5 Corwin, "Leadership as Pain-Bearing," 16.
6 Adeyemo, "Servant Leadership in an African Context," 4.

diverting this poison, poor leaders pass it on to the flock. Through passing it on they bring blame, creating suspicion, negativity, and discouragement among community members. This often results in destroyed relationships.

Pain breaks us. But as it tears our hearts open, it opens them up for Jesus to pour his cleansing blood in and for the Holy Spirit to spread his healing ointment. Only God can heal this depth of hurt. This is like the medicine that Jeremiah yearns for (Jer 8:21–22). Through this brokenness comes healing, resilience, and humility. It brings greater compassion and patience with people, and develops the wisdom of age and experience in contrast to the brashness of youth.

Moses is our great example of this. Not only did he have to come to terms with his own failure as a young man, he was broken by the complaints of the people he led. But he took these to God, and in his brokenness and humility found the strength to keep going. He consistently passed the criticisms and negativity on to God. Pain is, perhaps, God's way of keeping leaders grounded, and therefore humble.

Painful, difficult, challenging experiences are unavoidable for leaders. These situations are like a crucible refining leaders' character. It is human nature to avoid pain and difficulty. But good leaders embrace the cost of doing what is difficult for the sake of what they are responsible for. This takes courage.

Courage is determination to do what is right despite personal cost. Courage is a decision to act for the sake of achieving the group's vision or purpose and preserving the honor of God's name.

Mainstream secular theories of leadership development affirm that challenging experiences help people become more effective leaders. Beyond developing the capacity to absorb pain and embrace cost, challenging experiences cause us to question our current ways of doing things. They can prompt us to look for new ways of dealing with problems, especially when we have good support from other people.[7] Interacting with peers and mentors can help leaders clarify and then adopt these new perspectives and heart attitudes.

Support from peers helps us grow through trials. Developers should be alert for leaders who are wrestling with personal, family, or ministry challenges and give them opportunities to share their struggles either with developers or with a group of fellow leaders. Leaders feel supported as their problems are listened to with empathy. Their peers (and developers) affirm, comfort, encourage, correct, counsel, pray for them, and give concrete support.

---

7 Van Velsor and McCauley, "Introduction: Our View of Leadership Development."

Model Integrity and Transparency

Integrity means there is complete consistency between what leaders say and what they do. It also means consistency with the vision of the community. Leaders are a living reference for the community's vision. Paul regards integrity as essential for deacons: "In the same way, deacons must be well respected and *have integrity*" (1 Tim 3:8; emphasis ours). Integrity relates closely to faithfulness in the sense of unchanging commitment. Leaders model and promote consistency between values and behavior.

Leaders with integrity act in a principled way, even in difficult situations. Christian leaders' principles are based on biblical standards. They act according to their principles regardless of personal cost. Because they stick to their principles, there is no inconsistency between their actions in different situations. There is no discrepancy in the way they act in different roles, for example between being a husband, father, teacher, or tradesman. Similarly, their words and actions match up.[8]

Jesus described one of his first disciples, Nathanael, as "a man of complete integrity" (John 1:47). He was a man without "deceit" (John 1:47 NIV). Nathanael had no secret agendas. Leaders like Nathanael do not deceive or dissemble (to give a false or misleading appearance; to disguise one's true motives). What they say to different people or how they act toward them is consistent. They do not say one thing while aiming for something else. The leader's "yes" means "yes" in all dimensions: words, nonverbal communication, actions, and attitudes, and in all contexts. Integrity, therefore, creates a climate of trust because followers know that leaders are not plotting behind their backs. The leaders are not saying one thing to some people, but something else to others.

Leaders with integrity also respect the integrity of their followers. That is, they consider integrity an essential element of good character and will not try to force followers to act contrary to their principles. They will seek congruence between the values of the community and individual members' values. Where congruence does not yet exist, these leaders respect others enough to give time for congruence to develop.

For example, some young adults can be quite rigid in their interpretation of biblical statements and quick to judge others who do not act in conformity with their rigid interpretation. It can be difficult for these young adults to accept the fuzziness and messiness of what it means to "love one another." Leaders with integrity, while modeling the value of

---
8 Banks and Ledbetter, *Reviewing Leadership*, 102–3.

"loving one another," will value the integrity that underpins young adults' rigidity, while gently trying to soften their perspective.

Integrity is essential for resilience and health, as it provides a buffer in the face of accusation, complaints, and the changing views people have of the leader. Unlike James's "wave of the sea that is blown and tossed by the wind" (Jas 1:6), leaders with integrity are stabilized by their principles.

Integrity, through its stabilizing principles and consistency, also results in transparency. Leaders with integrity welcome inquiry, because nothing is secret. They are not afraid of exposure. Leaders with integrity nurture open, healthy communities. Followers feel safe because they don't have to fear hidden agendas that might cause them harm. They know the leaders' actions will always match their words and that their behavior is consistent with the leaders' personal values and the values the community espouses. As followers copy leaders' integrity, this produces transparency and health across the community.

Transparency allows problems to be discussed honestly. Leaders with integrity aren't afraid of the truth or different perspectives because of the confidence they place in their guiding principles. If there are problems, leaders are honest about them with followers. They don't try to hide the truth to make themselves appear in a better light. Transparency around the leader creates security in the community. Security comes from confidence in predictability about how the leader acts and makes decisions.

> ENABLE LEADERS TO BUILD OPEN, HEALTHY COMMUNITIES.

Personal integrity means accepting our own strengths and weaknesses. This honest self-awareness means that leaders are not threatened by others' strengths. Nor do they feel the need to protect or hide their own inadequacies. Paul advises all disciples: "Don't think you are better than you really are. Be honest in your evaluation of yourselves, measuring yourselves by the faith God has given us" (Rom 12:3).

Being honest with ourselves about our weaknesses helps us to be more ready to learn from others. We are more likely to actively seek out and value their expertise.

Corruption is the opposite of integrity. Power seduces leaders to compromise principles and transparency. When corrupted, leaders pretend to follow rules and expectations while secretly pursuing their own agendas. Like corruption, manipulation is also the opposite of integrity. It depends on deceit to make people do things, sometimes even things that destroy their own integrity (things that go against their own beliefs and values). Corrupt, manipulative leaders subvert the purpose of leadership to a hidden, self-seeking agenda, rather than to be an exemplary disciple who fosters fullness of life in the group.

Support God's Forging of Christian Character

Leaders' growing experience of God is the source of their continuing transformation toward Christlikeness year by year. Leaders who preserve a vital fellowship with God bear fruit, especially by growing in key qualities of character such as obedience to God and being willing to suffer for Christ (John 15:1–21; Gal 5:22–23). As Edgar Elliston and J. Timothy Kauffman observe, "Effective ministry emerges out of the quality of character—not out of technical competence."[9] This quality of character is forged in the crucible of daily life and fellowship with God.

God begins the work of character transformation at conversion, and he continues to build on that initial work year by year through the various phases of the leader's life (Phil 1:6). Leadership-development efforts are therefore just one contribution to the much bigger school of God which lasts throughout a believer's lifetime.

Spiritual formation is our response to the initiating work of the Holy Spirit to grow in our experience of God and Christlikeness. We cultivate individual spirituality through spiritual disciplines. These disciplines include daily reading or listening to and meditating on the Bible, prayer, silence, and solitude. It also has a communal dimension. The Holy Spirit uses other believers and their gifts to help form each person. Engaging with our community tests and further develops our maturity.

Christian-community relationships are critical to character growth. We grow through seeing mature Christians we can imitate. We receive nurturing support from relationships and learn through conflicts. Growth happens most when believers are free to use their spiritual gifts and God-given abilities to practice the one-another commands of Scripture (e.g., John 13:34). We learn and grow as we build one another up. If we, as developers, are in the community with leaders, we can model how to empower, encourage, and build up other believers. Part of modeling involves explaining why we act in the way we do. In this way, developers can be developing not just leaders but also affirming and helping to develop a spiritually formative community for all disciples.

The Lord uses adversity to develop Christian character. Suffering and difficulties help people grow in perseverance and endurance, Christlike

---
9 Elliston and Kauffman, *Developing Leaders for Urban Ministries*, 165.

character, and maturity (cf. Rom 5:3–5; Jas 1:2–4). Part of all disciples' spiritual development is learning to embrace rather than avoid difficulties. All disciples also need to grow in learning how to support one another in the difficulties and challenges of life. The best place to learn and grow in these things is in normal community in real life.

Conflicts are unavoidable. They arise within any group of leaders, between leaders and followers, between followers, and between leaders and developers. They are normal to life in a broken world. They are a great opportunity for growth. They help us learn to confess, forgive, be forgiven, and be reconciled. Conflict in the community also provides a good opportunity to learn about pain-bearing and how to manage it. Through pain and conflict, we develop resilience and courage.

It is wrong to think that developers can *train* people to be Christlike.[10] This is God's work. He transforms people, not us (Rom 12:2). Whatever we do in developing leaders should contribute to God's continuing work to cause the likeness of Christ to be developed in them (cf. Gal 4:19). We must be alert to resist the temptation to develop them into our own image, even while we are trying to be models worthy of imitation. This is a tricky balance to keep when working across cultures. We are used to doing things like spending time with God in ways that fit our own backgrounds. We only overcome this by being self-reflective and holding our own practices loosely. It also helps to have other people around us to model alternatives and challenge us.

We develop leaders' Christlikeness and resilience by supporting them through real-life difficult experiences, not by trying to break them in artificial community experiences. Developing leaders in genuine, community-based contexts guards against the risk of spiritual abuse. It is never acceptable for developers to break trainees; that is God's work alone. It is never acceptable, in any community, for leaders (or trainers) to manipulate people or to force participants to compromise their integrity.

Spiritual abuse occurs when trainers put themselves in the place of God to control or dominate trainees, overriding their feelings and opinions and causing harm to trainees' well-being and relationship with God.[11] There should be transparency about what is happening, and integrity for all participants. There is never any excuse for different

---

10 This point is well made in the Lausanne Movement's "Cape Town Commitment" in section 3 on Christ-centred leaders. This can be found at https://www.lausanne.org/content/ctc/ctcommitment#p2-4.

11 David Johnson and Jeffrey VanVonderen, *Subtle Power of Spiritual Abuse*, 20–21.

standards of character formation for developers compared to leaders. If developers are unwilling to be personally evaluated by leaders, they have no special right to evaluate leaders' spirituality. We are all Jesus's disciples, equally accountable before him.

As developers, we should encourage leaders to take responsibility for their own spiritual vitality and walk with God. At the same time, we can help them to experience a range of ways to draw close to God. They can draw on these for the rest of their lives. People with weak group orientation can benefit from learning to appreciate group spiritual-growth disciplines, such as daily meetings. People with strong group orientation can benefit from learning individual disciplines, such as personal reflection.

Be Examples[12]

We should strengthen leaders' ties with their local community for their own spiritual formation. Too often, leaders see their role as giving spiritual teaching and direction. They forget they have much to learn. They have a mutual learning relationship with their siblings in Christ. As developers, we too should be engaging with the local community, valuing their input into our lives. We should explain, as an example rather than a rule, what we are doing to grow in Christ and why we do these things.

> REMIND LEADERS TO KEEP LEARNING FROM THEIR COMMUNITIES.

A major thing that is good to model is how to respond to failure and conflict. By our response, we can help leaders see these as valuable learning opportunities. To do this, we need to be transparent about our own failures and conflicts. We should explain to leaders what happened and what we are doing in response. We can model healthy ways of resolving conflict and responding to failure, in ways that fit the local culture.

We should especially facilitate leaders' learning these things from mature disciples in the church. Sometimes, in a new church plant, mature believers are not available. Then developers can consult with the new believers. Together we can seek to understand the different dynamics in the conflict and how to apply the Bible to it. This creates a mutual learning opportunity to work out how best to respond in a way that brings reconciliation and healing to the community.

Developing godly character requires a more organic approach than can be defined by a pre-set program. It is demanding on developers. Because

---

12 Many of the following recommendations are drawn and/or adapted from Bernhard Ott, *Understanding and Developing Theological Education*, 6015–55, Kindle.

> IMMERSE YOURSELF IN THE LEADERS' COMMUNITY, SHARING EVERYDAY LIFE WITH THEM.

it is inseparable from real-life community, it is largely unpredictable. Developers have to be alert for opportunities to mentor and foster spiritual growth. This is how Jesus developed his disciples. It is best done by being immersed in the same community as leaders and investing in them life to life, day by day. This means spending much informal time with leaders. It includes eating together, visiting them in their homes, opening our own homes, relaxing, and serving God together in ministry.

A missionary friend assigned to provide biblical training to a group of evangelists and local church pastors in East Africa said, "I realized that you've got to include people in whatever you're doing as often as you can. For example, have people along with you in the car and talk through issues with them, and then do ministry together. This was the best training and influence that I was able to give."[13]

Many church planters and disciple-makers will already be doing this but may not have seen it as leadership development. The effect of being alongside leaders over the longer term will be more lasting than any program of study.

The International Council for Evangelical Theological Education stresses the importance of holistic leader development:

> We must look for a spiritual development centered in total commitment to the lordship of Christ, progressively worked out by the power of the Spirit into every department of life. We must devote as much time and care and structural designing to facilitate this type of growth as we readily and rightly provide for cognitive growth.[14]

Pentecostal missionary and missiologist Melvin Hodges pointed out that evangelicals too often "train the mind but fail to lead students towards spiritual maturity."[15] A Christian worker in China echoes this concern. He writes that pastors are pursuing degrees but have "lost something of the zeal and simple dependence on God that was a hallmark of the previous generation of leaders."[16]

---

13 Interview with Richard Hibbert, July 28, 2017.
14 ICETE, "Manifesto on the Renewal of Evangelical Theological Education," point 7: "Integrated programme."
15 Hodges, *Indigenous Church*, 58.
16 Fulton, "Beyond Theological Education."

After all, the writer of Ecclesiastes concluded:

> Be careful, for writing books is endless, and much study wears you out. That's the whole story. Here now is my final conclusion: Fear God and obey his commands, for this is everyone's duty. (Eccl 12:12–13)

The Cape Town Commitment expresses the shared position of over four thousand leaders who attended the Lausanne Movement's 2010 congress on world evangelization. Like the 2002 ICETE (International Council for Evangelical Theological Education) statement, this more recent document urges developers to do all they can to make spiritual formation a major focus of leadership development.

> We strongly encourage seminaries, and all those who deliver leadership training programmes, to focus more on spiritual and character formation, not only on imparting knowledge or grading performance, and we heartily rejoice in those that already do so as part of comprehensive "whole person" leadership development.[17]

We need to resist overemphasizing knowledge in our approach to spiritual formation. This can be difficult because we default to reproducing what we have experienced.

There is no single way of helping leaders grow in Christ that always works for every person. Christian leaders in every culture are usually familiar with core practices such as prayer and Bible reading. But they often are not familiar with the variety of other spiritual disciplines. Spiritual disciplines are intentional practices, relationships, and experiences that help people get to know God better and grow in Christ.

Luke lists the fundamental spiritual disciplines in Acts 2:42. Adele Calhoun reminds us that the first believers

> devoted themselves to the apostles' teaching [a practice] and to the fellowship [relationships], to the breaking of bread [an experience] and to prayer [another practice].[18]

It is good to engage leaders in these foundational disciplines together. It is also helpful to model, teach, and share each other's experience of additional disciplines. Spiritual disciplines help us draw close to God, hear from him, and respond to him. We should expose leaders to a balance of individual and communal spiritual disciplines. Examples of

---

17 Lausanne Movement, "Cape Town Commitment," section 3, Christ-centred leaders.

18 This is how Calhoun describes spiritual disciplines in her excellent handbook, *Spiritual Disciplines Handbook: Practices That Transform Us*, page 17. In it she explains how to engage in scores of different disciplines, connects each discipline to a particular dimension of character or spirituality in which the person would like to grow, and outlines the fruit of the discipline.

other disciplines are gratitude, celebration, practicing the presence of God, fasting, journaling, waiting, silence, spiritual friendship, devotional reading of Scripture, meditation on Scripture, contemplative prayer, and prayer walking.[19]

Different people have different pathways through which they experience God most readily.[20] Just as individual believers differ, so there are variations from culture to culture in the main ways that Christians draw close to God.

Reflecting on his experience of growing up and later serving as a missionary in Papua New Guinea, Kirk Franklin explains that his life experience with Melanesian Christians has deeply shaped his own spirituality. Practices such as many hours of praying together with leaders, expecting the Holy Spirit to transform and heal, and extended sessions of confession of sin and reconciliation between Christians became a norm for him.[21]

We cannot separate spiritual formation from action. God gives us the privilege of friendship with him. With this comes the responsibility to share our experience with others. God brought us into his kingdom to fulfil the work he prepared for us to do (Eph 2:10). He has given us his "wonderful message of reconciliation. So we are Christ's ambassadors; God is making his appeal through us. We speak for Christ when we plead, 'Come back to God!'" (2 Cor 5:19b–20).

It is the leader's role to empower and facilitate the local church to fulfil its part in that purpose. In chapter 10 we discuss how we can help leaders clarify that purpose and communicate it clearly to followers.

---

19 This is just a small sample of the options described by Calhoun in her *Spiritual Disciplines Handbook*.
20 The concept of different preferred pathways to experiencing God is explored and explained in more detail in Gary Thomas, *Sacred Pathways*.
21 Franklin, "Culture Does Affect Our Spirituality."

Chapter 10

Clarify the Community's Purpose (C3)

Four tasks of clarity are important for leaders. The first is to see the current situation clearly. The second is to picture a potential state (vision) clearly. Having clarified where the group is heading, the next step is to clearly identify the priorities toward achieving the vision (or purpose). Finally, leaders communicate clearly to motivate followers to work together to see the vision fulfilled or even exceeded.

The more compellingly leaders communicate vision, the more they inspire followers to want to contribute to its creation. Compelling means that leaders enable followers to clearly "see" something they all, together, want and are willing to pay the cost of achieving. This means that leaders are catalysts toward crafting something new. Without unifying, compelling vision, groups stagnate, or their members move in multiple directions and the group loses its cohesion.

Promote Clear Vision

Vision can be simple. Sometimes organizations have beautifully presented, grand visions, but these are rarely fulfilled. The best visions are simple. Everyone in the community can communicate them easily. God gave the Israelites a simple vision: "Everyone will live in peace and prosperity, enjoying their own grapevines and fig trees" (Mic 4:4). Its power is in what the simple image implies: peace, secure ownership of the land through the generations, sufficiency of food, and justice according to God's laws.

The purpose of a group, and therefore its vision, must be relevant to its local situation. We cannot just transplant a vision from somewhere else. It has to emerge out of the local context and speak to local people's emotions and needs.

Vision is central to community health and growth. It is key to the community's identity. When the people of Israel were about to move into the promised land, God gave them a vision. It was of a community blessed by the Lord. They would live a long time in the land. They would multiply as they wholeheartedly loved and served him (Deut 30:15–20). Choosing to aim for God's vision was a choice to pursue life and God's blessing rather than death and disaster (v. 15). From that point on, despite their repeated turning away from him, God consistently held before them this same vision of life and blessing under his rule, if they returned to him.

Vision implies and inspires change. Clear vision communication means hearers understand how they will change. They are clear on what they can do to bring change or influence for it. This vision inspires the group to grow into something better than they are now.

> EMPOWER LEADERS TO CATALYZE SOMETHING NEW.

For churches, what they will grow into is already largely clear from the Bible. Jesus commanded Christians to make disciples and grow the church. But the specifics of the vision depend on the local context. This includes what making disciples looks like. The patterns of growing the church (e.g., house churches, cell churches, megachurch) and what healthy churches look like will change in different localities. The vision may also define how the church impacts its local context in other ways (e.g., education, justice, alleviation of poverty, politics).

The terms *vision* and *purpose* are largely interchangeable. Vision expresses purpose in a way that group members can "see." Vision makes purpose more concrete for group members, so they are clear about what they are trying to achieve.

For the purpose of transforming a local slum, there might be several pictures in the vision. It might include people reading the Bible together, and sharing food and possessions. It could include children attending school with their own shoes and textbooks, safe electricity lines and clean water flowing into every home. It could be an overflowing Sunday meeting. These pictures help leaders and group members know what, specifically, they are aiming for in the transformation.

Christian leadership has a distinctive purpose in contrast to secular leadership. The vision of every Christian group, and its leadership, must line up with God's big-picture purposes for the world. It must help fulfill Jesus's promise of building his church, and filling the whole earth with the knowledge of the glory of the Lord (Hab 2:14; Matt 6:10; 16:18; John 10:10; 1 Cor 15:24–28; Rev 5:9–10; 11:15).

This grand vision of our Lord is fulfilled as people become and grow as Jesus's followers. Christian leadership's distinctive is therefore disciple-making. To assess how well we, as leaders, are doing in working toward God's vision, we can ask ourselves this question: "To what extent are we and the people we are responsible for growing deeper in our relationship with Jesus and bringing others into his kingdom?"

It is good for Christian leaders to reflect periodically on whether their leadership is resulting in people hearing the gospel, becoming more like Jesus, and actively trying to introduce others to him. If this is not happening, their leadership is not Christian, however effective they may be in general leadership terms.

Clarity of vision helps leaders navigate more easily through the myriad decisions they have to make with or for the group. Clarity helps leaders weigh up competing demands and decision results. This is especially helpful when it isn't possible to consult with others. It also helps community members keep their focus on what has the best chance of contributing to the vision. Leaders who don't clearly identify the group's purpose are often ineffectual in decision-making because they don't know what to prioritize. Sometimes they avoid making decisions at all.

Not having the personal ability to craft vision does not disqualify a leader from leading. Some leaders are adept at drawing vision out from others, or recognizing it when they hear others present it. Leaders may express a personal vision first. Or others in the group may first give voice to it.

Through his extensive research on teams, Meredith Belbin identified two ways in which leaders lead: either from the front, as Shapers, or from the middle, as Coordinators.[1] Belbin's model is valid and useful across cultures.[2] Shaper leaders have a clear picture of how to achieve vision. They stride out ahead to show the way, acting like a beacon that draws followers behind. The Shaper is the more typical image of the Western leader who says, "Follow me."[3] Coordinators stay with the group, gathering

---

[1] These descriptions are adapted from Belbin, "Belbin Team Role Descriptions," https://www.belbin.com/media/3471/belbin-team-role-descriptions-2022.pdf, and "Belbin Team Roles in a Nutshell," https://www.belbin.com/media/3309/belbin-team-roles-in-a-nutshell.pdf.

[2] Belbin, "Belbin and Culture Report," https://www.belbin.com/media/1935/belbin-white-paper-culture-and-belbin-team-roles.pdf; Swailes and Senior, "Belbin's Team Role Model."

[3] Western leadership theory has often focused on Shaper-type leaders. The dominant nineteenth-century theory of leadership focused on "Great Men" who moved history forward. Much later, a still popular theory of leadership—James MacGregor Burns's idea of Transformational Leadership in *Leadership*, 1st ed. (New York: Harper & Row, 1978)—envisaged a Shaper-type leader who is charismatic and entrepreneurial and who brings change through his own example and by communicating an energizing vision and challenging goals. Many books have been written to help such leaders get people to adopt and embrace the change that the leader wants to bring.

people around them, saying, "Come with me." Coordinators gather people, help them clarify goals together, identify, use, and praise people's abilities, and encourage them to work with the leader to achieve the group's vision.

Shapers and Coordinators work with vision in different ways. Both may craft vision individually or receive it from group members. Shapers are more likely to craft vision individually. They naturally look out beyond where the group is. Shapers are good at "doing" vision, which means crafting vision and understanding what is necessary to make that vision reality. Coordinators more often draw vision from the group. Coordinators are good at facilitating others crafting vision and working out how to fulfill it.

Either way, leaders embrace the vision and enable others to embrace it also. Wherever the vision comes from, good leaders communicate it continually and effectively. They hold the group accountable for its fulfillment.

While the vision might be a clear picture, leaders need wisdom to know how that vision applies to day-to-day situations and their transformation. They need the Holy Spirit's wisdom to discern what God specifically wants. They also need to know how to draw on the wisdom of the community. They need to know how to search the Scriptures for answers to specific contextual problems and how to make biblical vision concrete in local everyday life. For example, if the vision is a community where everyone "loves one another," leaders need to be clear on what community members can specifically do to live out this biblical ideal. The leaders' role, in this case, is bringing clarity to followers about what "loving one another" means in concrete terms, both through words and personal example.

If they aren't living out a clear, transforming vision, groups begin to stagnate and eventually die. Organizations have a five-stage life cycle for growing and aging.[4] The first stage, the birth of the church or organization, is characterized by a strong vision communicated by a charismatic leader (or a church planter). During the next two stages of growth and maturing, the group's vision is still at the forefront and guides decisions. Structure develops to support its fulfilment. But in the final two stages of decline and breakup, rules, procedures, and bureaucracy sap the group's vitality. Vision fades into the background or is ignored as maintenance of the organization supplants transformation.

This correlates well with the second or third generation of believers in a church plant. The first generation know what they have come from and

---

4 Haire, "Biological Models"; Moberg, *Church as a Social Institution*, 118–24.

what they want the church to be. But the second generation rarely have the same compulsion to aspire to something greater. They settle into preserving the institutional structures of the church. As the third generation grows up, they struggle to see their grandparents' vision because their world has already been transformed. Without a compelling vision it is difficult for them to commit to the church. They often disengage or leave altogether.

In Japan, church growth and multiplication has generally been very slow. But a recent study of Japanese churches that continue to plant new churches affirms the importance of leaders having a clear vision. John Mehn studied six churches that were multiplying and that between them had planted sixty-two more churches. He found that the leaders who catalyzed churches reproducing shared certain characteristics. One characteristic common to all these leaders was a compelling, biblically rooted vision they felt they had received from God.[5]

Vision is not inanimate. It is alive in the sense that people embody it. Leaders embody the vision and become an example to the group of what fulfilling the vision looks like. How leaders embody the vision is the crux of their integrity. They inspire people to become the vision with them. When leaders have integrity, what they aspire to will match what they do.

If followers discover discrepancies between what the leader says they should be and what the leader does, this usually results in disillusionment. Often it also results in increasing group dysfunction, as healthy followers leave. These healthy followers abandon the group, either by physically leaving or by nonengagement, because they cannot trust the leaders to lead the group according to the group's intended purpose. Remaining followers may continue the unhealthy group because of conscientiousness. This is unhelpful because it perpetuates dysfunction. Or they may continue the group for personal gain. This can happen when they receive roles they are unqualified for as the healthy people leave. Again, this perpetuates dysfunction. Remaining followers may show an unhealthy dependence on the leader, increasing the unhealthiness of the group.

Help Leaders Craft Collective Vision

Developers can strengthen the way leaders consult with their communities about what the group believes God wants them to be transforming. A common approach used by Western trainers is brainstorming in small groups using words and drawings on large sheets of paper. This can be effective and efficient, but often neglects the critical step of analyzing the

---
5 Mehn, "What Kind of Leaders Reproduce Churches?"

responses, discerning God's voice, and crafting a coherent vision from this. Often, leaders just compile what everyone says to make a confused "vision." It is simply everyone's thoughts and agendas added together. Other times, leaders ignore everything people have said. They superimpose their own agenda or vision.

In cultures where face-to-face brainstorming may be more challenging, leaders will often garner group members' views through talking with different people outside any large group meeting. It is the leaders' responsibility to bring coherence to multiple views of what the community should be aiming for, leading to a clear communal focus.

Crafting coherent vision from multiple views is a complex task. Leaders need several skills. These include analysis and synthesis of different viewpoints. They need to be able to manage the group consultation process and summarize what the group has said succinctly. They need spiritual discernment. The best way to learn these skills is through doing them with a mentor present. The mentor can encourage, guide, and model, as needed. It is important that the way the consultation is done fits the local culture.

In strongly group-oriented cultures, developers need to first research how group consultation occurs in the local context and then strengthen the leaders' skills in gathering community members' views. Vision emergence in this context is likely to take more time than in weak group-oriented, democratic approaches. As community members talk with one another and with leaders, eventually a consensus emerges. Leaders may make suggestions to influence the discussion according to different issues. But they have to be patient, giving the time for the community, as a whole, to decide what its vision is. If community consultation is short-circuited, the community will continue as it always has, ignoring the vision the leader imposes.

> ALLOW TRANSFORMATION TO BE EXPRESSED IN CULTURALLY FITTING WAYS.

Vision relates to transforming from one state to another. This is affected by how we perceive time. Like every attempt to explain differences between cultures, the explanations we offer here about how cultures differ in their orientation to time are rough sketches. They are a bit like doorways through which we can begin to understand more of the uniqueness of the people we serve, in this case their distinctive way of understanding time.[6]

---

[6] Information about differing culturally shaped views of time has been drawn from the following sources: Hiebert, *Transforming Worldviews*, 50–54; Graham, "Role of Perception of Time in Consumer Research"; Zimbardo and Boyd, "Putting Time in Perspective"; Lee, Liu, and Hu, "Relationship between Future Time Orientation and Item Nonresponse."

People's orientation to time is deeply ingrained and we are not usually aware of it. Edward Hall called a group's view of time their "silent language."⁷ It operates at the deepest level of how people make sense of their world, so it can be difficult to uncover. A group's time orientation points to what they spend most of their time thinking about—the past, the present, or the future. It is important to understand leaders' view of time before we try to help them with vision. For example, there is no point in insisting on a ten-year plan when the community has little interest in the future.

People in Anglo-European cultures usually have a linear view of time. These countries also score highly on future-orientation in the GLOBE study. Mediterranean countries were lower down the scale, and non-Western countries had the lowest future-orientation. People with a linear orientation to time see time as being like a road that stretches from the past into the future. Activities are steps on a line toward future goals. Time, and events within time, advance in a set chronological order. Being clear on chronological order is highly valued.

Figure 7: Vision in linear time

In this cultural view, vision improves on what is happening today or what happened in the past. Every moment of time is valued. It is an opportunity for improving oneself or the world. Time can be used well or wasted. To help Anglo-Europeans use time well, clocks, watches, and timetables are found everywhere in their societies. Figure 7 represents the linear view of time. In these cultures, the idea of a strategic plan that includes chronologically defined steps (time-oriented goals) in working toward that vision makes sense.

Many people from cultures in Asia, Latin America, and the Pacific Islands see time as being circular or repeating. The author of Ecclesiastes communicated this view: "History merely repeats itself. It has all been done before. Nothing under the sun is truly new" (Eccl 1:9). According to this view of time, the same events repeat cyclically. Time does not stretch into a new future. People expect a future that is just like the past. They therefore focus on the present and the problems that each day brings. What is done today does not change the future state. Figure 8 represents this view of time.

---
7 Hall, *Silent Language*.

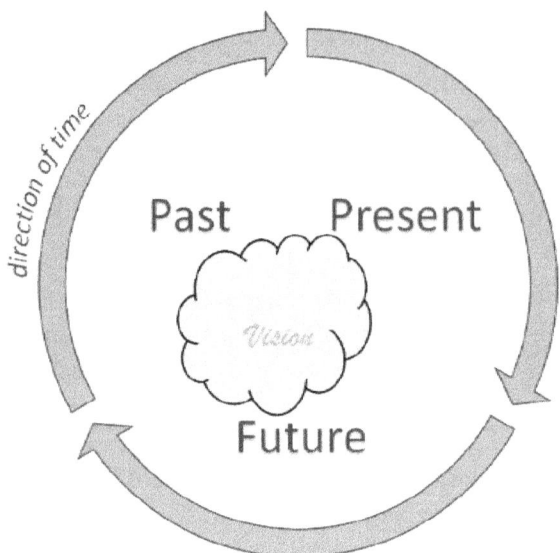

Figure 8: Vision in cyclical time

Millet culture is present-oriented. The order in which events happen is not important for them. When they tell a story to recount an event, such as explaining how they came to faith in Christ, they merge events into the ever-present today. As linear-time thinkers listening to Millet testimonies, we found it very hard to make sense of their stories because we often could not understand the order of events. We sometimes spent a long time asking them questions to try to unravel the chronology of events in their stories. The sequence of events is not important to the Millet storyteller. Instead, their prime concern is how these events affect their current experience of God.

Vision for present-oriented people who live in an ever-repeating today does not have the same sense of permanence as for people who think of time as linear with a focus on the future. Only the repeating cycle of the seasons or natural events has permanence.

For leaders in present-cyclical time cultures, vision is a picture of something that may have previously existed in some form and will likely exist again in the future. The length of chronological time between a past and present state is unimportant. The best way to communicate vision in these contexts is by using concrete, everyday, and present experience rather than an abstract picture of the future. Connections with previous similar experiences should be highlighted.

When we asked the Millet about their vision for their churches, we found that they focused on their experience at the start of the people movement to Christ, expecting it to repeat into the future. They had a very clear picture of their love for one another and the warmth they felt as the Holy Spirit moved miraculously among them. Their vision was more than just a drawing on paper. It encompassed the concrete actions expressed in community relationships and the feelings they experienced together. They were not interested in imagining a new future. They referenced the past as part of present and future experience.

Many people in sub-Saharan Africa, South Asia, and East Asia direct most of their attention to the past. They look to the past as a foundation for all present and future events. Ancestors are still present and active in daily life, so it is important for people to take their ancestors' wishes and values into account when making decisions.

In past-oriented cultures, time flows from the present back into the past. Figure 9 represents this. African theologian John Mbiti explains that there are two types of future events for Africans. The first type is unavoidable but predictable, such as natural events (seasons, storms, floods, droughts). The second type is currently unknown, indistinct, and yet-to-be-experienced events. The second type is not important to the traditional African leader.[8]

Scott Moreau uses the analogy of a person standing in a river facing downstream to explain this African view of time. People can see the water flowing past them (the present) and the water which has flowed past them (the past). But they can see very little upstream water. Since they feel they cannot influence the flow of the river upstream, they see no point in trying to control it.[9]

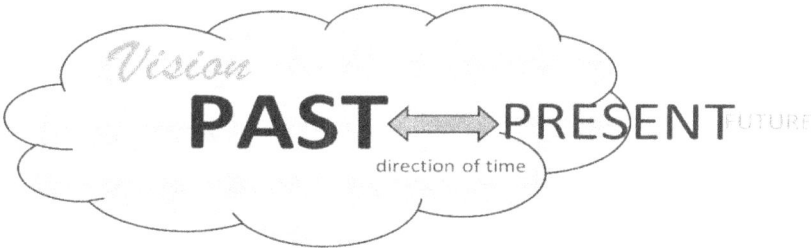

Figure 9: Vision focused on the past

---

8 Mbiti, *African Religions and Philosophy*.
9 Moreau, "Critique of John Mbiti's Understanding."

For past-oriented people, vision must anchor in the ideal past. If the vision does not reflect the past, it has minimal value. This also happens in the Bible's view of time. Even though the Bible makes it clear the past was not ideal, it uses past events to show how God's people should be living today and in the future. Examples of this are the new heavens, new earth, and new Jerusalem, which God will create (Rev 21:1–2), God referring to himself as the God of Abraham, Isaac, and Jacob, and the continual references to previous kings as a standard for judging succeeding kings in Chronicles. These are central to God's vision for the future, yet each builds on and is rooted in the past.

We find all three views of time—future-oriented, present-oriented, and past-oriented—in the biblical record. Whichever culture we come from can influence us to think that God's view of time fits with our own. But God does not act only according to one conception of time. He is above time. He created it. Yet he also entered it. Sometimes God roots future vision in what he has done in the past. At other times he highlights the glory and permanence of the future. It is other than what we have experienced (e.g., Rom 8:18–30; 1 Cor 15:35–55). Elsewhere in Scripture, God's focus is on the everyday fellowship God's people have with him in the present (e.g., John 15:1–17).

Encourage Clear Communication

Vision is more than a picture. It has to inspire feelings that motivate people to action. When we asked the Millet to describe a healthy church, they had a very consistent picture of what this looks like—everyone loving one another. They contextualized this into the emotion of "warmth." They looked back to the beginning of the Millet movement, when "there was a lot of warmth. We looked out for each other and visited each other. We met frequently. We sang songs and hymns passionately. We were always praying for each other."[10] The desire to reexperience the warmth inspired them to action.

Communicating vision is a creative process. It evokes emotions. Creative arts, including word pictures and audiovisual media, are the best way to communicate it. Creative media like stories, pictures, songs, proverbs, dances, and video all have the potential to communicate more than words alone. Vision that does not evoke a strong affective (emotional) response is unlikely to motivate people to achieve it.

---

10 Hibbert and Hibbert, "Diagnosing Church Health across Cultures," 250.

Leaders also need to outline how, together, the group can achieve the vision. That is, leaders clearly explain what each person needs to do. A great vision is all very well, but if the steps to achieving it are not clear, or are unrealistic, people soon opt out. If the vision is clear and the leader does not live it, or cannot make people's achieving it easy, this usually results in followers' frustration and disillusionment. If people don't know what to aim for, or how to get there, they give up. They look for alternatives to give their energy to.

Leaders inspire both by communicating the vision and by showing followers, by example, how they can achieve it. As followers set out to achieve the vision, leaders also encourage and empower followers in their work toward the vision.

An outstanding example of a leader with vision in the Bible is Nehemiah. His vision was simple: a restored wall completed around Jerusalem. Nehemiah communicated the vision to the people in Jerusalem. He gave them clear and achievable steps toward its fulfilment. He lived the vision by joining in building the wall. He empowered the people by providing resources, an example, and encouragement. He held them accountable for their contributions and celebrated the project's final achievement with them.

Leaders need freedom to express vision creatively in locally meaningful ways. Developers may encourage leaders to create pictures or make vision statements like those developers are familiar with from their own training and culture. Instead, it is better not to impose foreign means of creative expression on leaders and their communities. Vision is a creative process, and creativity flourishes when given freedom.

GIVE FREEDOM FOR CREATIVITY.

Encourage Vision Review

However clear the vision is, it needs to be adjusted as circumstances change. Changes may occur in the context or in the group. It's important that leaders are alert for these shifts and remain responsive to them. To do this, leaders need to be regularly interacting both with people in surrounding society and with group members. They need to reflect on what they observe. The quality of the leaders' reflection will be improved as they seek out and listen carefully to a diversity of voices.

Failing to do this was the mistake that Solomon's son Rehoboam made when he only listened to the voices of his peers and ignored the older men. Both groups had helpful perspectives. If Rehoboam had learned to evaluate the experiences of both groups, he might have reached a more balanced vision of what his kingdom could have looked like post-Solomon (1 Kgs 12:1–19; 1 Chr 10).

Leaders repeatedly have to review the vision as group expectations change. While in the desert, the Israelites were greatly disappointed and frustrated with the time it took to fulfill the vision of entering the Promised Land. Out of their frustration, they complained to Moses. Moses repeatedly had to manage their expectations, recommunicate the vision, and deal with his own emotional responses. In the incident of Moses striking the rock at Meribah (Exod 17:1–7), Moses's angry response to the community's endless complaints resulted in his missing out on seeing the vision's fulfilment.

As they age, organizations, including churches, become increasingly focused on preserving the status quo. They resist adjusting the vision, even if the surrounding context has changed significantly. The vision loses its connection to the surrounding context. This becomes a self-perpetuating problem as the group appoints leaders who are good at preserving the status quo but poor at "reading the times" and bringing change.

The Pharisees in Jesus's time are a good example of this. The Pharisees were well-educated in God's law; and thus they knew to expect the Messiah. But they were so busy looking at the texts and theory of the Messiah, they failed to recognize the living Messiah among them. If they had listened to the Holy Spirit and the people's voices, they would have renewed their vision for the future of Israel. They would have adjusted their vision according to a new perspective of what the community of God's people could be. Leaders who focus on "doing things like they have always been done" exclude leaders who bring fresh vision. They resist being accountable for achieving vision as conditions change in the local context.

As human beings, we normally prefer to gather opinions that affirm what we already think. It takes discipline to seek out different and opposing viewpoints and to listen carefully to them. Age is helpful here, because older people are more likely to have experienced opposing viewpoints and outcomes. It is normal for younger people to be more confident in their views. They tend to have a more simplistic view of issues. Experience tempers our opinions. However, experience doesn't always result in openness to different viewpoints. Sometimes it cements narrow-mindedness when people refuse to engage with alternative perspectives.

As developers, our role is to help leaders appreciate the importance of evaluating multiple perspectives and proactively seeking them out. We also need to help them learn how to arrive at conclusions.

Otherwise, bewilderment at the multiplicity of perspectives can result in paralysis. We therefore should help leaders develop skills in listening, consulting, and promoting discussion between people with conflicting opinions. We can model for them how to weigh up conflicting viewpoints and discern the way forward. We do this by making our thinking explicit by explaining it out loud.

We need to help leaders find balance between the vision, accountability for helping the group to achieve it, and the group's circumstances. A common mistake in individualistic Christian leadership is that leaders personally assume all the responsibility for achieving vision, which effectively excludes the group. Often this happens because the leader thinks the group lacks interest or commitment. Leaders feel like they have to carry the vision alone and drag everyone along behind them.

When Moses lost his temper at Meribah, he fell into the error of taking all the responsibility onto himself. Just as he didn't have the power to make the water flow, he likewise couldn't make the people follow God. When the Israelites left Egypt, they, with Moses, committed to the vision of entering the Promised Land. This joint commitment broke down whenever the group saw Moses as solely responsible for its fulfilment. It also failed when Moses took the responsibility onto himself rather than handing it over to God (which he was normally very good at doing). Any breakdown between the group's and the leader's common responsibility needs to be addressed.

Jesus commanded his disciples to show the world that they are his disciples through the way they love one another. This is Jesus's vision for his church. Each community of disciples lives this out in a specific cultural context. To fulfill Jesus's vision, the community needs culturally fitting accountability. This helps to ensure a balance between the leader's and the community members' responsibility, as well as recognition of God's role in making the greater-than-expected happen. In chapter 11 we explore how the group lives out its collective responsibility.

Chapter 11

Develop Care Across the Community (C4)

Jesus told the Twelve that their love for one another was *the* sign to the watching world that they belonged to him (John 13:34–35). Importantly, it is the disciples' love *for one another* that distinguishes them as people who belong to Jesus. He did not highlight just one disciple's—the leader's—caring for everyone, but every disciple's caring for all the others. Jesus envisaged a community distinguished by the quality of its relationships. This is an outstanding characteristic of the Acts 2:44–45 community.

The church is a collective, a single community, a "one-another-ness," not just a set of individuals. Writing as individualists, we stress how difficult it is for individualists to truly understand this. We only came to appreciate it when we experienced it as the Millet wholeheartedly embraced us into their way of living. A true community is more than the sum of its individual members. A new identity comes into being.

Paul communicated this idea with the images of a building (1 Cor 3:9–17; Eph 2:19–22) and a body (1 Cor 12:1–27). A building is more than just a stack of bricks. Its interconnected structure protects and supports each part. As a temple, it provides a communal space for meeting with God. A body is also more than its individual parts. Each interconnected part brings life to other parts, as well as to the whole.

Sometimes people think of the biblical body image like a factory, where each part does its set task on an assembly line. But a body is organic and not easily separated into its mechanistic parts. Life is in the interconnectedness. A building only comes into being and remains standing when the interconnections support the whole structure. The interconnections nurture fullness of life. They bring the affective experience of joy, fulfilment, security, encouragement, and belonging. These are all intrinsic to healthy togetherness.

Lift Up Carers

The idea of a solo leader caring for his flock is inseparable from an expectation that leaders solely care for the needs of each individual. In larger churches, care might be delegated to sub-leaders. This can unintentionally communicate that care is of less importance. This one-to-each-one-of-many idea of care, flowing from the leader to every single follower, undermines the Bible's ideal of believers loving one another.

> NURTURE INTERCONNECTEDNESS.

When the community hands the duty of care over to a single leader, this puts an overwhelming load on that leader. Too often, it leads to burnout as he tries serially—one individual after another—to care for each person's needs. It can result in severe frustration for the leader. He realizes he has been given an impossible task and resents that others do not help out enough.

Essentially, people outsource their biblical responsibility by paying a pastor. By accepting this, leaders unintentionally communicate that disciples can substitute money for personal responsibility. We need to counter this message by shifting leaders' focus to the community as a whole, and members' focus to their one-another duties.

Christian leaders are called to be examples to their communities of "living a life of love," just as Jesus did (Eph 5:2). They follow in Jesus's footsteps, who provided the supreme example of what it means to care for people (John 3:16; John 13:1; 1 John 3:16). But their example is as a disciple who is a carer, one among many.

The most commonly used passage to teach how we should care for one another is the incident of Jesus washing his disciples' feet (John 13:1–17). Jesus used this one-off incident as an object lesson to reinforce to his disciples that they were all equal in their subservient status under him, their Teacher, Lord, and Master. Jesus stressed that "slaves are not greater than their master. Nor is the messenger more important than the one who sends the message" (John 13:16). He repeated the same lesson about humility over and over to his disciples.

Scripture records two other incidents of foot-washing, both done by women (Luke 7:36–50; Matt 26:6–13; Mark 14:3–9; John 12:2–8). Jesus rebukes Simon, the Pharisee, for his condemnation of the woman who washed Jesus's feet with her tears when Simon had failed to extend that courtesy himself. Both Matthew and Mark highlight the significance of this incident. They both record Jesus stating,

I tell you the truth, wherever the Good News is preached throughout the world, this woman's deed will be remembered and discussed. (Matt 26:13; Mark 14:9)

Many women of the world, including Millet women, still continue to wash the feet of their husbands and visitors. The practicalities of loving one another is not extraordinary for most women in the church. Their faithful caring is simply unacknowledged.

By washing his disciples' feet, Jesus highlighted the taken-for-granted service of women and servants or slaves. He made their invisible, faithful service a normative standard for care. He wanted his disciples to imitate him as he imitated women and household servants or slaves. In doing this, he set a standard for humility according to the actions of people the disciples hardly noticed.

Like Jesus, let's help leaders open their eyes and see those who serve. Let's resist any tendency to count them as less than the leaders themselves. The standard for one-another care then becomes those who naturally care.

> HIGHLIGHT TAKEN-FOR-GRANTED SERVICE AS THE STANDARD FOR ONE-ANOTHER CARE.

It is clear the twelve disciples did not take Jesus's foot-washing lesson literally. They were quick to hand over practical serving responsibilities to others in the growing church in Jerusalem (Acts 6:1–6). The dispute between Greek-speaking and Hebrew-speaking believers about widows' food was a test of the one-another-ness of the community. The leaders intervened for the sake of preserving harmony and ensuring the welfare of the whole community. The twelve disciples kept the well-being of the whole community in focus. They also accepted that they, as leaders, could not do everything.

Nurture Healthy Relationships

It is rare to see Jesus portrayed in Scripture without groups of people surrounding him. Similarly, his disciples were almost always together in twos, threes, or larger groups. When Jesus speaks to single disciples (e.g., Peter after the resurrection), it is a brief aside out of the group of disciples. Similarly, individuals who meet Jesus one-on-one—such as the Samaritan woman at the well (John 4:1–42)—are quick to introduce him to their community. Although Nicodemus came to see Jesus on his own, in secret (John 3:1–21), we later see him with his peers, the Pharisees (John 7:45–52), and burying Jesus's body with Joseph of Arimathea (John 19:38–42).

When people who are not Christians come into church communities, their experience should be better than in other kinds of groups. Thankfully, this is often the case. Several Muslim-background believers have told us that visiting a church was a major turning point for them. They saw the way Christians related to one another. It was different from their Muslim communities. One friend told Richard, "I could see there was no backbiting. These people really cared about each other."

But neither should we assume that we cannot find good relationships in non-Christian communities. Sometimes, in fact, non-Christian communities do better than Christians. It is good to accept this in humility and strive to do better.

Jesus said, "My purpose is to give them a rich and satisfying life" (John 10:10). God intends local churches to be communities that are flourishing and full of joy. He wants participants to enjoy each other's company because their relationships are satisfying and nurturing. Christian leaders' role is to foster this flourishing life.

The greatest challenge to healthy, nurturing Christian community is broken relationships. Sin, unforgiveness, and conflict are unavoidable in any group, including churches. John teaches us what to do when we sin in 1 John 1:8–10. That conflict was a continuing reality in the early churches is clear through Paul and Barnabas's disagreement (Acts 15:36–39). Paul and Barnabas conflicted with Christian leaders from Judea (Acts 15:1–2) and believers in Corinth (in both letters to the Corinthian church). Believers conflicted with one another in the same church (Phil 4:2–3).

> OVERCOME CONFLICT THROUGH COMMUNICATION AND RELATIONSHIP REPAIR.

Health does not mean no sin or conflict. Christians nurture health when they cooperate with the Holy Spirit to resolve conflict and deal with sin. This means that leaders need to be able to deal with sin and conflict within the church community.

In a healthy Christian community believers live (or walk) in the light of God, who is light (1 John 1:5–7). Walking in the light means being honest about our sin, confessing it, asking for forgiveness, and forgiving those who have hurt us. It means being quick to deal with sin once we become aware of it.

Ananias and Sapphira did the opposite of this when they tried to cover up their actions and so deceive the community (Acts 5:1–11). They walked in darkness. The leaders' role was to expose the darkness and give them the opportunity to confess what they had done. By continuing to try to cover up what they had done, they broke the trust between people in the group. If God, through the apostles, had not dealt with this, community members would have started questioning what one another said. They would have become suspicious of one another. We learn transparency by seeing it modeled for us.

Conflict may not be because of sin, but it always damages relationships. Conflict is overcome through communication and repairing the broken relationships. Different cultures manage conflict in different ways. Some cultures use words and direct confrontation. Other cultures prefer indirect communication and mediators. Because conflict is often highly emotional, some cultures focus mainly on addressing the emotional barriers that conflict creates between people. They often do this using food and gifts.[1]

All these methods can be found in the Bible. As developers, we need to research how to manage conflict well in the culture. Then, we can help leaders hone their conflict-management skills in culturally sensitive ways.

Barnabas the encourager is an outstanding example of a leader whom the Holy Spirit gifted to build and nurture healthy Christian relationships and communities. He consistently worked to mend broken relationships and to give people an opportunity to restore themselves after failure. We see this first in the way he reached out to the newly converted Saul. Although all the other believers did not trust Saul and were still afraid of what he might do to them, Barnabas sought him out and reconciled him with the others (Acts 9:26–27).

We see it again when the Jerusalem church selected him to go and encourage the new Gentile church in Antioch (Acts 11:22–24). We also see it in his wanting to give Mark another chance to redeem himself on a second missionary journey (Acts 15:36–39). As developers, we should seek to be like Barnabas, encouraging and restoring leaders, and supporting them as they do the same for others.

Nurturing healthy relationships is critical to making the community safe for all its members. A safe community is characterized by mutual respect between members, including acceptance of diversity. Conflict is managed well. This means members are not afraid to express differences of opinion. All members are confident that their voice

> VALUE DIVERSITY AND DIFFERENCE OF OPINION.

---
1 We explain some of these different cultural ways of managing conflict in "Managing Conflict in a Multicultural Team."

will be heard in community discussions. They know that difference is valued, not suppressed. Caring in this way means proactively valuing each member and ensuring their voices are heard and respected.

In a safe community, people can make mistakes and even fail. Failure is seen as an opportunity for learning, with leaders modeling healthy responses to failure, including admitting and apologizing for mistakes. In this kind of community, people feel free to try new things and to learn from their experience. For such a community to develop, members must trust the leader and one another. Members feel cared for because even when they make mistakes, they know they will still belong and feel accepted by everyone in the community.

Share Life Together

The disciples felt Jesus's closeness through the years they spent with him. The Lord Jesus left his exalted position in heaven to live among humanity as a human being (John 1:1, 14). He drew close to people in their need. He especially drew close to the Twelve, calling them to be with him so they could experience life together (Mark 3:13). Following in Jesus's footsteps, leaders who care for people draw close to them. This means leaders and followers are walking together on the Jesus Road. Leaders are not separated into an exclusive group.

> HELP THE COMMUNITY AND ITS LEADERS TO MUTUALLY SUPPORT EACH OTHER.

Jesus not only gave care; he also received it. This underlined his humanity, his closeness to others in his human needs. With his disciples, he was served by a group of women who cared for their basic needs, such as food. He received love from friends like Lazarus, Martha, and Mary. Receiving from others empowers the givers and builds mutuality within the community. In the Acts 2 community and in Paul's interaction with churches, we see both giving and receiving.

In a community where relationships are healthy, members serve one another through hospitality. They forgive, help, and support one another in every part of their lives—materially, mentally, and in spiritual growth. If leaders keep themselves apart, either because of pride or a misguided desire not to burden others, they break this mutual one-another-ness. We have heard people say that leaders can't have friends in their congregations. This is harmful, as it isolates leaders. It denies them an essential part of what it means to be human and to belong in a community.

When difficulties and challenges arise, fellow believers with relevant spiritual gifting share the responsibility for finding solutions with the leaders. This spreads the burden of problem-solving across the community. It protects leaders from being overwhelmed or crushed. Leadership development, therefore, needs to strengthen both leader and community. It should also develop their interdependence, ensuring they support each other well.

Leadership development that encourages leaders to keep themselves apart from their communities or to see themselves as superior will break the disciples-together bond that is necessary for mutual care between leaders and followers. Leaders are then likely to see themselves as above needing the advice, support, or help of "ordinary" believers. Believers also lose motivation to care for their leaders.

A Christian community cares for its leaders for the sake of the overall purpose of the community. This purpose is to make disciples and extend God's kingdom on earth. Care that does not contribute to this purpose is nonessential. For example, leaders do not have to receive salaries so they can work full-time for the community. It may be better for leaders to continue working in secular jobs part- or full-time. If the whole community is living for Christ, leaders' material needs may be no greater than other community members' needs. These members work in secular jobs, actively share their faith, and serve their Lord according to their gifts.

> BUILD COMMUNITY THAT CONTRIBUTES TO AND RECEIVES FROM OTHERS IN ITS CONTEXT.

Healthy communities interact with their contexts. They have healthy links with other people and organizations around them. This is in contrast to cults or sects, in which members close themselves off so no one knows what is happening within them. This means leaders care for their communities by managing relations with other groups. They foster good relationships between their community and other communities, encouraging members to engage respectfully with people outside their church. As they interact, healthy groups also foster life in their engagement with others. This helps to prevent isolation and keep a healthy, balanced perspective of the world around them.

Good leaders believe the healthy, life-giving nature of their own community can add value to the world around them and empower members to spread the life of Jesus beyond the group's borders. Having a healthy perspective means leaders respect what people outside the group have to offer. They are willing to learn from others' perspectives and help the group to respond fittingly to the surrounding world. In this way, leaders build a resilient community that contributes to and receives from other people in its context.

Coordinate Believers' Gifts

God gives every believer spiritual gifts to build up the community of God's people. Only some receive a Romans 12:8 gift of leadership.[2] Every member plays an essential part in the community. "A spiritual gift is given to each of us so we can help each other" (1 Cor 12:7). Leaders' responsibility is to help members discover their God-given gifts, roles and the work God has prepared for them to do.

Leaders help the roles and gifts work together effectively to fulfill God's purpose for the community. The Apostle Paul mentions five kinds of leaders—apostles, prophets, evangelists, pastors, and teachers—but his key point is that they are tasked with equipping God's people to build up the church. He writes, "Their responsibility is to equip God's people to do his work and build up the church, the body of Christ" (Eph 4:12).

As is true of every facet of the leaders' work, this does not mean that the whole responsibility for identifying members' gifts lies with them. The community can identify and will affirm individual gifts and roles if leaders allow and empower them to do so. We recognize that the Holy Spirit is at work in every believer.

Leaders need to be alert for members who are sidelined or excluded. This is one way that leaders put into practice their responsibility to watch over the *whole* group. Like Barnabas, they can encourage those who lack confidence or who are overlooked by more dominant group members. Leaders ensure that all members are given their rightful place and voice in the community, along with opportunities to use their gifts. Again, the leaders' focus is caring for the community as a whole. If some parts of the body are excluded or suffer, the whole body is negatively affected (1 Cor 12:26).

People either *feel* cared for or they don't. Many aspects of community life may cause either a feeling of belonging and well-being, or a feeling of being devalued. People can be offended by the smallest and simplest of unexpected things and yet be unmoved by major issues.

Communication is the key skill that leaders need to grow in. Communication allows leaders to help people explain what they are feeling and why. Needless to say, people communicate differently in different

---

2 See Plueddemann's discussion of this in *Leading across Cultures*, 173.

cultures. Developers need to be sensitive to this, because otherwise they may train leaders in skills that are counterproductive to communication in their context.

When leaders empower every believer to use their gifts, they open the way for disciples, leaders, small groups, and churches to multiply. Leaders who are instrumental in helping churches multiply want every believer to excel in using his or her gifts for the building up (which includes multiplication) of the church and the extension of God's kingdom. These kinds of leaders raise up and release many more leaders.

Moses displayed this attitude when Joshua protested about the Holy Spirit being given to other leaders in the camp. Moses was glad for others to receive power to serve God and the people. He was very happy for them to share in his experience of God (Num 11:16–30). Humility is not self-abasement, but rather delighting when others develop in their experience and service of God. In Moses's case, he also understood that the whole community would benefit from the empowering of more people to lead.

Julyan Lidstone worked for decades in Western and Central Asia. An Iranian friend of his excitedly came to him after reading that Jesus wanted and promised that his disciples would do even greater works than he had done (John 14:12). He had been used to leaders who made sure that their followers never surpassed them and therefore threatened their own position. He was "astonished that a great leader like Jesus would want his disciples to excel in this way."[3]

Build the Local Community

As we spend time with leaders in their communities, we can model what it means to encourage community members individually and as a group. This includes explicitly valuing all the members of the communities we are engaging with. To "explicitly value" means to say specifically good things about people and what they do. To do this, we need to live life with them in their communities, sharing our daily lives.

> EXPLICITLY VALUE PEOPLE BY SAYING SPECIFICALLY GOOD THINGS ABOUT THEM.

Being in the community alongside leaders means that we can both give and receive care from community members, modeling how to do this well. It also provides an opportunity for leaders to see us in our human weakness, as we show that we too need others. Locals will be quick to see whether we truly consider ourselves part of the one-another relationships

---
3 Lidstone, *Give Up the Purple*, 74.

of the community or think we are better than them. What we model will be reproduced in the leaders we develop.

Often, extracting leaders from their communities—for example, by taking them away for several years to a residential Bible college—is justified by the value of learning in a college community. It is true that leaders can develop relational skills from interacting in a college community. But they have less responsibility for the college relationships than in their own communities. In their church, they have to be a living example of Jesus's intended one-another-ness. In the college community, teachers are the examples. The challenges in the extracted community are also unlikely to be as demanding as the real-life crises of daily life in the home church community.

Leadership development focuses on strengthening one-another caring within the community, building the community while developing the leaders' relational skills. Developers can help leaders learn how to identify and affirm existing community strengths, including members' gifts and abilities. The most effective way of doing this is for developers to live in the community, personally modeling how to do it.

Leaders will also need training and mentoring in how to build a safe community. Developers can help leaders look for people with less voice, access to resources, or power. These are the "weakest" members of Christ's body and those who seem "least important." Paul directs us to give them special attention (1 Cor 12:14–25).

To put this into practice, developers must help leaders identify disempowered, excluded, or vulnerable members of the community. Developers can mentor leaders to increase the voice and participation of marginalized and weaker community members. In our own attitudes and manner, we should model valuing each person in the community.

Unresolved conflict is usually the main impediment to healthy community life. The first step in helping others to develop conflict-management skills is to help leaders identify good ways of managing conflict according to local cultural approaches. Start with real-life examples of conflict. This helps to make the skill-training relevant and will also help in understanding the complexity of the issues involved.

It is often helpful to role-play ways of managing conflict outside of a real-life situation first. Role-playing in a safe environment helps us identify our emotions, consider reactions from other participants, and prepare different ways of responding. In role-playing, learners take on the roles of different people and respond to one another as authentically as possible.

For example, leaders might role-play resolving a major conflict between several church members. The more participants give themselves to the role, the better the learning experience is. It is important to encourage leaders to feel and speak the same way people in that situation would. This helps leaders to learn to recognize and manage their feelings when they face them in real life. Role-playing also allows us to experiment with alternative ways of responding, and to receive feedback on what we do.

> HELP LEADERS RECOGNIZE AND MANAGE THEIR FEELINGS.

Role-plays and simulations are especially helpful for learning how to manage emotions and develop scripts for difficult interactions. This is because, in the heat of the interaction, we often don't know what to say or how to act. Role-plays also enable participants to debrief in a safe context. Ideally, as a final step, leaders then practice their skills in real life, preferably with a mentor's support.

Up to this point in the book, we have compared leaders with disciples, discussed how culture affects leadership, and examined the four critical characteristics of Christian leadership in some depth. In chapter 12, we focus specifically on the developer.

Chapter 12

What Should We, as Developers, Do?

Build Relationships

Leadership development is, first of all, an interpersonal relationship. The most important factors are people. Leadership development is about developers, leaders, and communities.

The quality of leader development depends on the people. It reflects the quality of both developers and leaders, and the quality of the relationships between them. Great curriculum, wonderful facilities, and excellent resources will not develop leaders if the interaction between developers and leaders is poor. Leaders might receive interesting cognitive stimulation and learn how to write an essay well, but there will be minimal transforming of leaders' communities. In contrast, a leadership-development program with poor curriculum, next-to-no facilities, and negligible resources can have a deep impact on leaders. This occurs when developers invest their lives into quality relationships with those leaders.

Because leader development is a reproductive task, we reproduce ourselves whether we mean to or not. We become reproducing models. Lecturers produce people who speak at others, focusing on information transfer. Developers who take a group of leaders with them, as they visit homes and share the gospel in their communities, produce leaders who visit homes and share the gospel in their communities. As developers, therefore, we need to reflect upon what our lives model and how we can intentionally model what we would like to develop. This is the 2 Timothy 2:2 principle that Paul passed on to Timothy. Paul's whole life was a model for Timothy to reproduce in those who followed him.

> BE INTENTIONAL ABOUT WHAT YOU REPRODUCE.

As people choose to follow leaders, they give leaders influence over them. In the same way, leaders choose to be influenced by developers. We influence not just by what we say but through our relationships and the example of our lives. People relate to people. We are embodied. We feel emotion and physical pain. We get tired, stressed, anxious, and live with others who similarly experience the strains of normal life.

> MODEL HUMANNESS RATHER THAN PERFECTION.

It is through the weaknesses of our embodied humanity, through our sin and failings, that we most powerfully model what it means to be both disciples and leaders. This means that we need to let leaders see our humanity rather than a mask of perfection.

The most effective way of influencing is by sharing our lives. That means going with, doing with, being with, pushing forward with leaders while supporting them. We encourage from the background and are there to debrief, listen to, and share their pain as they learn through the unpredictability and messiness of real life.

Preferably, developers emerge out of personal church planting and experience in leading churches in the same cultural context as the leaders. If we would like leaders, for example, to learn how to manage conflict effectively, the best way is to be with them in the conflict that occurs in their ministry contexts. How can we truly understand all the factors, people, stresses, and culturally fitting methods of managing conflict if we have not experienced it? Ideally, we have experienced and managed the same types of conflict.

If we want leaders to be transparent about money and other challenges, how do we become vulnerable in ways that match their vulnerability? If we are developing leaders where churches are rapidly multiplying, how can we possibly appreciate the chaos and the pressures on the leaders if we have not been immersed in that context? It made a big difference to the Millet leaders we related to that we had planted a church in a difficult area of Bulgaria. They knew that we had lived the same struggles that they had.

Be Models

Again, to be models means being in the leaders' context with them. It means living among them, engaging in the same daily activities and ministries. It means sharing our lives with them, including family life. To be models, we have to be seen. And the model needs to be relevant for the context.

The word *model* is often used as a verb for teaching skills. Here we use *model* as an example of how to live life as a leader in a holistic way, fully immersed in a specific local community. As part of living life as a leader, we model leadership skills. A model is a living reference for how to be a leader amid daily life and ministry.

Just as all leaders are first of all disciples, so developers are also first of all disciples. *Disciples* is a community term. All followers of Jesus belong to the community of Christ. We grow together in character, the fruit of the Spirit, and obedience to God's Word. We show that we are Jesus's disciples by loving one another. We hold one another accountable for the honor of God's name.

Developers must be exemplary disciples, living in the leaders' community in such a way that our lives can be an example to other disciples. This does not mean that we need to pretend to be perfect. Rather, in our humanity we show how to live for Jesus. We become living references who are examples of how to think and behave in different situations.

Modeling is a whole-of-life "activity." As living references, we model as whole people. When leaders think about what to do in specific situations, they will refer back to memories of developers in similar situations. They extrapolate from this how the developers might have thought and behaved. The better leaders know developers, the more they will be able to imagine developers' responses.

We, as developers, should be modeling living out the 4 Cs. We should be part of the leaders' community, humbly respecting and valuing each member, and building up the community as a whole. It is likely that we will engage with more than one church community. We need to be consistent in our attitudes and behaviors toward each person and his or her community.

Local people will quickly pick up on our prejudices. We should develop our capacity to listen to diverse people, reflect on our own attitudes and behaviors, and be quick to admit faults and ask for forgiveness. If we are open to learn, and value challenges and failures as opportunities to learn and grow, we will be more successful in developing leaders who reflect these important traits. We should be clear about the purposes of the communities we are engaging with, promoting them clearly and living them out passionately alongside local leaders. We should give and receive. Through this, we model interdependence as well as the importance of each person in the community.

As a model, we live out our daily lives and do ministry, but also intentionally explain why we do or think what we do. In this way, we make our decisions and judgments explicit for

> MODEL YOUR THINKING BY SAYING IT OUT LOUD.

leaders. We help them to understand why we choose to act in certain ways, what our attitudes are, and how we manage our emotions. Our modeling extends beyond our actions to include our inner thinking and reasoning.

Sometimes this is difficult to do. However, it also benefits us. It forces us to reflect on why we are thinking, acting, or reacting in particular ways. Doing this opens us up to learn from and be accountable to leaders and other disciples. This helps us grow in maturity. This, in turn, becomes a model for leaders in how they can be models for others.

Coming from another culture, there will be some things we do that are outside the experience of life in the local context. Some examples of this are home leaves and conference attendance. Other things may be very different than local practices—for example, how we raise our children. Sharing our lives as models means investing the time to explain these differences, making the reasons for them transparent. In doing so, we model transparency. Respecting local leaders as adults means assuming they will understand if we make the effort to explain in a meaningful way.

Mentoring is different from modeling. It intentionally focuses on specific skills or issues. Developers or leaders can initiate mentoring. In the West, it is often done with regular hourly appointments based solely on reports by leaders. Mentoring is more effective if developers and leaders are together in ministry. Mentors can then give advice and support immediately. They can also demonstrate alternative ways of approaching what is happening. When developers see the leader in ministry, they can raise questions about things leaders may not have noticed. Developers also evaluate according to direct observations rather than second-hand interpretations.

Leadership development is a collaborative process. Often, we think we are going to change people, but God intends for us to learn more than we give.[1] We work together with the people God has chosen and filled with his Spirit to build his church. It is a mutual task. We must constantly remind ourselves of this mutuality and resist assuming we are the only people with anything to give.

> BE READY TO RECEIVE.

Research the Culture

The best way to learn about the culture is to spend time living among the people and learning their language. As we live in a community, we get to know the people as individuals, families, and groups. We learn about the relationships between them and the stresses on them. We learn what

---
1 See Johnson, *We Are Not the Hero*.

individuals' and the community's strengths are and how best to encourage and affirm these. Through more specific research, we can learn about indigenous patterns of leadership. Throughout this book we have explored many aspects of culture which would be helpful for developers to research. In this section, we list these.

Apart from researching more obvious things about leadership, such as describing what good leaders look like and how leaders are selected and appointed, other areas of culture strongly affect leadership. Questions that help us to learn about these areas are listed below.

Group Structure and Belonging

- Map the groups that leaders belong to, researching the boundaries (e.g., how group members are selected or excluded) and interactions between groups, and the power of each group over other groups.
- How important is group identity?
- What is the power distance between leaders and followers?
- Is there any ranking in the right to speak?

Group Control over Members and Leaders

- To what degree is behavior and self-worth affected by community opinion?
- What are the terms of any social contracts between leaders and followers?
- What local systems support leaders in their growth, keep them accountable to the community, and protect them from vulnerability to power and riches?
- How do people in the local culture try to protect leaders and their communities from abuse of power?
- How do people in the local culture manage communal resources well? What causes mismanagement? How do they protect the community and leaders from mismanagement? What does the community do when mismanagement occurs? How do they resolve the problem?

Group Discussion Processes

- How do families make decisions? Who takes the lead? Is there discussion?
- How does group consultation occur?
- What is the role of the leader in group consultations or discussions?

Power

- Who are the most influential people in the community? (These may include media and national as well as local figures.)
- How do leaders gain power?
- How do they use their power? How do they influence people?
- What does power feel like for leaders and for those who experience its abuse?

Conflict

- How is conflict managed well?
- How do families settle quarrels?

Uncertainty

- How important is it for the group to feel that the unknown is under control?

Wisdom

- Who is considered wise?
- How have wise people gained their wisdom? If there are recognized scholars or religious teachers in the community, how have they gained that recognition?

Words

- How important are words in relationships and in relation to other contextual factors?

Education

- What are the leaders' and followers' levels of
    - o Education
    - o Literacy
    - o Majority-language skill?
- What are the leaders' and followers' expectations of education generally and leadership development specifically?
- What different agendas do different groups of people have for education generally and leadership development specifically?
- What is the leaders' degree of preference for oral methods of learning?
- What technologies are local people comfortable with using for communication? What are the limits of these for teaching and learning?

Time
- How is time viewed?
- What is the range of time for which it is acceptable to come to or leave a meeting or class? What reasons make it acceptable to be late or leave early?

Contextualize

> WORK ON LETTING GO AND LETTING GOD BE IN CONTROL.

Our role as developers is to help local believers evaluate local practices. They decide about how to live their faith authentically in their own context. We have to control our tendency to assume we know best. We need to be careful not to dominate or manipulate the discussion to cause the believers to decide that what we think is the best option, rather than allowing them to make their own decisions.

This is the case even if we disagree with what they decide. We need to cultivate humility, respect, and trust in God's work in his people. We need to learn to "let go and let God" be in control, and to interrupt our assumption that we understand better than others. Essentially, we shift our view of ourselves as developers who tell people how to follow God to fellow learners who are discovering together with local people what it means to follow Jesus in their locality.

We need to learn how to facilitate discussion in culturally fitting ways. When we think about consultation, we probably imagine a Western democratic meeting. If this is how local people normally consult, we would focus on ensuring that all members of the group can share their thoughts. We would be alert for any excluded members due to biases in the group. However, if consultation is done differently in this culture, we should facilitate consultation in the local way. This, for example, might mean taking the time to do much small-group discussion at different times and then facilitating local leaders presenting the conclusions to the larger group.

It can be helpful to research the cultural meaning of what will be discussed before we facilitate consultation. This is because most people don't think deeply about why they do what they do. These deep meanings usually only emerge when others violate their values. Our role is not to tell participants what we think the meaning is, but rather to ask questions that help them ponder deeper meanings if they aren't used to thinking like this. An example of how to do this is to describe an incident which provoked a major reaction and explore with the group why this reaction occurred.

Similarly, to help local people evaluate practices in the light of the Bible, Christian traditions, and Christian experience in other settings, we can present options to explore rather than dictating what we consider is relevant. For example, if we are working in a new church plant and believers don't yet know their Bibles well, it is tempting to tell them what the relevant passages are. But a better way might be first to explore what areas of Christian teaching or experience they think are relevant. Then we can suggest passages we think might be helpful. We allow believers to examine these passages themselves to discover whether they think they are relevant to the issues involved.

A good example in our own experience related to a Muslim thanksgiving sacrifice that new believers were spontaneously using in the church. On deeper exploration with believers about the meaning of the sacrifice, there was some ambiguity. They weren't convinced that Paul's teaching about meat offered to idols applied, even though the passage, at first glance, appeared relevant. They determined that the primary issue was not sacrifice but manipulation of God. Therefore, thanksgiving offerings brought to the church in gratitude for God's answering prayer were acceptable. They decided that thanksgiving offerings were okay as long as they weren't associated with a previous bargain made with God.

Adjust Our Methods and Expectations

Much of the world's population either cannot or do not regularly read. People who use the spoken word to communicate and rarely, if ever, use the written word are known as oral learners. People in many places where leaders need developing are oral learners. They rarely use reading to learn. Some oral learners can read but choose not to. Many oral learners can read well, while others cannot read at all. Instead, oral learners are those who receive, process, remember, and pass on information in oral ways. These ways of thinking and learning differ significantly from the ways used by print-preference learners.[2]

People's preference for either oral or print-based methods falls along a continuum. People who cannot read at all can only be trained, at least at first, using oral methods of teaching. Some leaders never learn to read. All their development occurs through listening to and memorizing stories, proverbs, and passages of Scripture. They learn through conversations, which include reflection on their experience in the light of what the Bible teaches. Others do learn to read and may learn to use print-based methods.

---
2 Madinger, "Will Our Message 'Stick'?"

Nevertheless, many people who do learn to read still prefer to learn using oral means and usually learn better through them. Even people who are highly trained in print-based learning will often learn more from oral methods. This is because these methods are more holistic and closer to lived experience. An important step for developers to take, then, is to assess leaders' degree of preference for oral methods of learning. Once we understand leaders' preference regarding oral versus print learning, we should adjust our approach to teaching the Bible to suit how leaders learn best. Many grassroots Bible-training institutes in Africa, Asia, and Latin America have adjusted their programs to suit the learning preferences of oral learners.[3] We can learn a lot from their experience.

> BRING THE LEARNING TO THE LEADERS (AND THEIR COMMUNITY) IN AN ACCESSIBLE WAY.

If we want leaders to learn specific cognitive knowledge, we need to make the learning accessible to them. This means it needs to be within geographical reach of them or in a form of distance education that they can manage, which helps them to learn. For example, simply putting written materials online does not mean leaders can learn from those materials. Many factors impact how useful those materials are for learning. These include simple things like electricity supply, access to computers and the Internet, and the navigational format and language of the learning software.

As a simple example, we ran a short course on interpreting the Bible in Moodle for a small group of Millet leaders. Although the course was in Turkish, they needed to sign up for Moodle via all the European data-protection permissions, which were only presented in English. We had to use screenshots and videos and get successful students to take the others through each step, helping one another to navigate an incomprehensible set of screens and buttons.

If we want to use online methods to communicate, teach, or pass on materials, the first thing to do is to research what the leaders are already using. We need to learn to use the apps, technologies, and materials that are familiar to them. As for all cross-cultural communication in ministry, the onus is on us to learn first rather than forcing learners into what we are comfortable with. It is quite possible that what leaders use has limited capacity, so we may need to adapt to those limits.

---

3 This book, by multiple authors, describes specifically how various training programs in Africa, Latin America, and India have adapted their approach to suit oral learners: Chiang and Lovejoy, eds., *Beyond Literate Western Contexts*.

Facebook, for example, is extremely limited for teaching and learning purposes, but it is widely used among the Millet. If we want to use another learning platform, we need to start with Facebook and build bridges to other platforms that are still accessible to the Millet. This means investing the time to adjust teaching and learning methods to the different learning platforms and technologies available, as well as helping learners to use them. We will also need to continue to support them as they use them. Again, our commitment is to their learning rather than just exposing them to written or audiovisual material or forcing them to learn in a way that we're comfortable with.

Too often we assume that just because we present (teach) something, leaders have learned it. Rarely is this the case. It is even less so when learners are unfamiliar with the language, culture, or method of presentation. Judith Lingenfelter points out that missionaries who are training leaders often assume that once learners have taken a course on leadership, they will be able to assume a leadership position. She helpfully notes that the first time many learners engage with a course, the main thing they are learning about is the teacher's unfamiliar style of teaching. The second time, they can better concentrate on the content. The third time, after observation and imitation of the teacher outside the classroom, they start to put the course into practice.[4] It is worth reflecting upon how many times Jesus had to repeat simple lessons to his disciples, and even then they didn't always get what he wanted them to learn.

Mediate

Imagine that you are developing a group of semiliterate minority-group church leaders. They speak two or three languages, but their formal education was in their second or third language and only went up to early high school. You are concerned about the continuing lack of respect these leaders receive for their achievements by denominational leaders. This is especially because only graduates of theological colleges are recognized as leaders by the denomination.

All ordained leaders of the denomination belong to the majority people group in the country. Your aim is to help these minority-group leaders develop their own relevant theology that addresses the major issues their communities struggle with. As an advocate and cultural mediator between the minority leaders and the majority group in control of the national church, you would like them to receive official recognition for their efforts.

---
4 Lingenfelter and Lingenfelter, *Teaching Cross-Culturally*, 630, Kindle.

Negotiation with a college for recognition requires much discussion of how language and culture affect education in majority-controlled contexts. Other important issues include oral versus literate approaches, individual versus collective learning, means of assessment, time lines, and student fees. All these exclude these minority-group leaders from successful participation in theological education. However, all these things could be addressed through careful educational advocacy and research-based evidence for change. This is beyond the scope of this book. But we wanted to include it for you to be aware that it is possible, even if rarely attempted.

As advocates for these leaders, we need to make the effort to try to negotiate pathways for them into ordination. We also need to work to create opportunities for them to have a voice alongside the dominant groups in institutions, including the church. It is not enough just to be an advocate. Once they come among the dominant group, they will need significant support to be successful within it. This advocacy is important for the sake of the minority groups' affirmation of their value before God. It is also important for dominant group members to have their perspectives challenged. Their understanding needs to be broadened to appreciate the richness of God's kingdom beyond their own cultural boundaries and blind spots.

> CREATE LEARNING PATHWAYS THAT SUPPORT AND AFFIRM ALL LEADERS.

For many years, Ashish Chrispal has been working to improve leadership-development efforts in Asia, especially in the form of theological schools. He points out that the majority of pastors and evangelists who are being trained come from marginalized and oppressed backgrounds. They have minimal school education. Yet they are the ones who speak the heart language of their people and who know their culture deeply.

Chrispal sees a stark mismatch between the training needs of these grassroots leaders and the way they are being trained in theological institutions. He asks, "Can we help people develop theological education that flourishes and takes shape in earthen vessels of different soils so that the living waters of the Lord may quench the thirst of many who are dying without Christ?"[5]

Let's do what we can to create learning pathways for these leaders that support and affirm them and enable them to have a voice in their own countries' churches, as well as the global church.

---

5 Chrispal, "Restoring Missional Vision in Theological Education."

Become Reflective Practitioners

Developers need to be reflective practitioners. This means cultivating the discipline of continuously reflecting on our assumptions, attitudes, and actions. It means continuing to learn all we can about the local culture, the Bible, and intercultural ministry. It means habitually asking questions about what we see rather than assuming we understand what is going on. In this way, we learn to monitor our attitudes and behavior, and continually evaluate the effectiveness of our ministry. To reflect, we need foils for our reflection, such as continual study of the Bible, and ministry experience and scholarship from the same and other cultural contexts.

If we consistently reflect on ourselves and what we do, this develops in us an openness to consider different ways of interpreting what we see and experience. It protects us from rushing into action based on false premises. It is helpful to have a friend or group to do this with. In discussion with others, we often discover perspectives which we would not have considered ourselves.

Having summarized what we, as developers, need to be and do, chapter 13 summarizes how to do leadership development using five principles as a guide. We conceptualize it as a holistic sharing-of-life together in a particular cultural context. We recommend drawing on problem-based modular training for specific leadership challenges, as these challenges emerge in the life and ministry of leaders.

Chapter 13

Leadership-Development Principles

This chapter answers the question: What are the essential elements of any leadership development we create?

We have distilled our answer into five principles:
1. Disciple leaders like all other disciples.
2. Select leaders who are endorsed by their communities.
3. Include the community around the leader and strengthen it.
4. Develop the 4 Cs.
5. Connect knowledge with experience.

As we recommend developing leaders using flexible, problem-based learning, we explain how to do this. But before launching into the principles, we consider where the development takes place and the importance of reproducibility.

Like for Jesus's disciples, the best place for learning is amid life, snatching teaching moments from the incidents that occur during each day. But to do this, developers need to be alongside leaders in their normal lives. This is not a good use of time or resources by Western standards. It depends on developers investing huge amounts of time with small numbers of leaders.

Jesus's knowledge curriculum probably could have been squashed into a six-month lecture series. However, it would not have had the same impact. Jesus's real-life teaching associated lessons with everyday objects and emotions that occurred as the disciples lived, walked, and worked with Jesus. For example, disciples would always associate living water with the sensation of drinking water from the well after the long walk to the Samaritan village (John 4:1–42). Peter would always associate not being afraid with Jesus pulling him out of the water in the middle of a storm. He would remember the panic of nearly drowning (Matt 14:22–33).

We cannot reproduce these powerful lessons in the sterile environment of a classroom.

We have to set up sustainable leadership development that is not dependent on external developers. If we don't build reproducibility into our approach, the leaders' development is likely to falter once the outsiders leave. This is regardless of the quality of the people or the approach. We need to focus on how to empower more permanent members of the community to continue without dependence on outsiders.

The basics of reproducibility are the cost, resources, and way the developing is done. DNA, which continuously reproduces itself, is the building block of life. When we start developing leaders, it is good to reflect on the DNA of our approach. We should evaluate whether that DNA can reproduce itself in the leaders' environment.

1. Disciple Leaders Like All Other Disciples

The first step in developing leaders is discipling the leaders as disciples, like all other disciples. There are no shortcuts to making disciples. However, the developer does not need to be the discipler. The local church does this best.

Leaders are disciples among disciples. They are not special disciples. They should not be separated out from other disciples. This increases their vulnerability. It makes them inclined to consider themselves better than others. Separation makes them more vulnerable to abuse their power. It tempts them to consider the community's resources as their personal benefit.

Therefore, the foundation of developing leaders is strong discipling across the whole community of believers. If most disciples are growing in Christ, it will soon become clear who the mature believers are. They will stand out by being examples for others. As all believers develop in understanding what it means to live for Christ, they become more able to support leaders in their leadership. They will also be confident to challenge them when they stray from what Jesus would do if he were leading in their cultural context.

All believers should keep on learning the Bible throughout their lives. All believers need to know their Bibles and put what the Bible says into practice in their lives. All believers are commanded to make new disciples and pass on to them what they have learned. New disciples then pass this on to more new disciples, in an unbroken chain until Jesus returns.

Being able to teach and guard the truth is not the exclusive domain of leaders. Gifted teachers who study the Scriptures in depth and are skilled at passing on what they learn may not be gifted leaders. The more all believers in the church know their Bibles, the truths of their faith, and how to live these out, the stronger the church will be. Learning the Bible is essential for all Jesus's disciples. It should be made as accessible as possible for *every* believer.

As developers, doing all we can to establish good discipling across the whole church may well be more important than developing leaders. A stronger church will naturally develop its leaders in a contextually fitting way. Let's encourage all believers to keep on learning the Bible and what scholars over the ages have decided are important truths for all believers. Our aim is for all believers to be like the Bereans, who "searched the Scriptures day after day to see if Paul and Silas were teaching the truth" (Acts 17:11).

2. Select Leaders Who Are Endorsed by Their Communities

Local people are the best judges of the character of disciples and their potential for leadership. Selecting disciples for leadership development should therefore be a consultative process weighted toward the opinions of mature disciples in the local church.

> LISTEN TO MATURE LOCAL DISCIPLES.

If there is no local church, or the group is still small, there is no need to rush to appoint leaders. Let them emerge in their own time. If they emerge naturally, they are more likely to have their community's support. This will help protect them from leaders' vulnerabilities. Paul left fledgling churches on their own and sent Timothy and Titus back to appoint leaders later. Churches in Antioch, Rome, Ephesus, and Berea developed their leaders independently. Being patient and giving time for disciples to be tested, and for leaders to emerge, protects against the tendency to extract young men from their communities. It keeps leaders embedded in their own communities, enabling leaders and churches to grow together.

Selecting leaders who are already leading means recognizing leaders of all types, especially small-group leaders. Mobilizing, encouraging, supporting, and developing small-group leaders in homes, neighborhoods, and workplaces empowers these new leaders to make disciples who make disciples. It affirms them in their ministry, which interfaces with the surrounding community. If we wait until churches are larger and require full-time, paid pastors, we devalue the leadership of the small-group leaders. We shift the focus from disciple-making to managing an institution.

3. Include the Community around the Leader and Strengthen It

GROW LEADERS AND CHURCHES TOGETHER.

The people in the leaders' home community know their leaders best. They will recognize and endorse (or otherwise) each leader's capacity for leadership. Because they know each leader well, they will be quicker to recognize problems. They also have culturally fitting, tested strategies for addressing those problems. They have the greatest vested interest in the leaders' development, because the results personally affect them. This means that we should broaden the focus of leader development to include the local Christian community the leader is part of.

We should include the community in creating leadership development. Community members know what kind of leaders the community is looking for. They are familiar with gaps in existing leaders' abilities and qualities. They will have expectations about the results they would like to see from the leader-development process.

Invite community members to join in training events or activities. We can also include them by making them developers. For example, a gifted teacher can mentor a leader to become a better teacher. We can encourage people who are good at managing conflict to model what they do and mentor leaders with less experience in this area.

To do this, developers need to be alert for people in the community who could develop leaders. We should ask the community to propose people who are skilled in particular areas. Often, because of power and hierarchical issues, people who are proposed feel inadequate compared with outside developers. In this case, we can be present but stay in the background. We should do what we can to facilitate the modeling of their skills. Including community members in this way reinforces that leaders are not superior to the rest of the community. It emphasizes that they are interdependent with community members.

If the community becomes more aware of the results of good leadership, they can work with leaders for success. The community can evaluate its leaders and their development. They are also a mirror for the effectiveness of the leaders' leadership.

Address Leaders' Vulnerabilities

To protect leaders and their communities from misuse of power and resources, we need to help them set up culturally fitting means of accountability. Research in the context will help developers to have some idea of what accountability structures should look like. We can facilitate leaders and followers consulting together to decide on a biblical way of holding leaders accountable that best fits the local context.

Developing leaders to address their vulnerabilities means developing the structures around leaders rather than just teaching leaders about them. Once leaders have experienced good accountability, especially if they helped set it up, they can help new leaders establish their own. The other advantage of doing it this way means that other people in the community also develop experience in and concrete ways of protecting and supporting leaders. They can help other leaders and their communities set up their own accountability structures.

Promote Leaders Learning How to Teach from Gifted Local Teachers

Paul told Timothy and Titus that church leaders need to be able to teach (1 Tim 3:2; Titus 1:9). The Bible lists teaching as a gift (Rom 12:7; 1 Cor 12:28; Eph 4:11). It gives many examples of people teaching without specifying whether they had the gift of teaching. Paul does not state that leaders need to have the gift of teaching, simply that they need to be able to teach.

Anyone can learn to teach well if they are willing to invest time and effort in learning teaching skills. One key to being a good teacher, and which characterizes gifted teachers, is the compulsion to learn. Gifted teachers get insights from the Bible and life. They communicate these in a way that results in changed lives. Teaching is not limited to preaching. There are many gifted teachers who quietly share their insights in their homes, in workplaces, and wherever groups gather. They markedly affect the lives of those who gather around them.

Just like all leaders are disciples but not all disciples are leaders, so all leaders should be able to teach but not all gifted teachers are leaders. But teachers are leader-like because teachers have significant influence over others. If we want to learn who the leaders are, we look to see who people are following. To find gifted teachers, we should look for people who are driven to learn the Bible and whose insights change learners' lives. Listen to who people say they are gaining biblical and life insights from. Who do they go to when they have questions? That is, don't just look for people who talk at the front of church meetings; look for the evidence of lives changed through the insights and equipping teachers pass on.

> FIND GIFTED LOCAL TEACHERS AND EMPOWER THEM TO TRAIN LEADERS TO TEACH.

To find gifted teachers, look for people who love learning. Look for those who naturally pass on what they learn to others. Take note of people we also learn from. They are likely to be the people who most naturally contextualize biblical truth to the local context. Remember, not all teachers can read. They may ask others to read for them. Or they listen more attentively than most to anything they can access. They will be good communicators, but not necessarily in foreign ways, like three-point sermons. In some contexts, for example, the best way to teach may be to lead a responsive song. In others, it may mean mentoring an apprentice.

Teaching occurs in many ways, not just from the front of a church meeting. We see Jesus teaching individuals and multiple sizes of groups right up to huge crowds. He taught in temples, on mountainsides, walking along the road, while eating, and in the middle of a storm on a boat in the center of a lake. Teachers tend to turn every situation into a learning opportunity.

Being able to teach means being able to learn, keep on learning, and pass on that learning effectively to others. The skills and techniques of teaching can be learned. They will depend on the context. If there are already gifted teachers in the church, the best approach for developing leaders' ability to teach is to facilitate these gifted teachers teaching the leaders. For us, as developers, it is good to watch and learn from excellent teachers in the local culture. This is important because the way they teach may be different from ways that are familiar to us. As we teach leaders to teach, we should—as much as possible—model local, reproducible ways of teaching. This affirms local ways of teaching rather than imposing ways of teaching from our own background.

> AFFIRM AND STRENGTHEN LOCAL WAYS OF TEACHING.

4. Develop the 4 Cs

Community

Community is the context in which leaders live and where we should develop leaders. Building community is a complex skill. We explain how to develop complex skills later in this chapter. We must continually discipline ourselves to widen our gaze so that whenever we consider leaders, we also consider the communities they are part of. We should actively resist any inclination to separate leaders from their communities, either physically or by giving them a status separate from or above other disciples. We show that we value communities by incorporating them into the way we think, talk, teach about, and train in leadership.

Character

The most powerful and effective way of developing character is through living examples. We become like the people we admire. People will follow our example whether we want them to or not, because of our position of influence over them. It is good to try to ensure that leaders have exposure to local examples as much as possible. In pioneer church-planting situations, this may not be possible. If the church is new and more experienced leaders are not available, we may be able to find mature leaders from churches close by. We might also be able to arrange for apprentice-style time with mature leaders close by. It is good to have exposure to several different living examples, as each person models different things out of their own uniqueness. This helps to affirm the value of the diversity within the body of Christ.

> EXPOSE LEADERS TO AS MANY LIVING EXEMPLARS AS POSSIBLE.

A second means of developing character, for all of us, is developing the discipline of continual reflection on our attitudes and behavior. The aim of reflection is to develop a habit of assessing our attitudes, motivations, and actions with the aim of continual improvement. We are trying to foster self-awareness and self-control, preferably in the moment rather than after the fact. Developers can model this through making their own self-reflection explicit. This means talking about what is going on in our thinking as we reflect on what we have said or done.

Modeling our inner thoughts means making them transparent. Making our thoughts explicit models how self-awareness and self-control affect our own attitudes and behavior, and the way we respond to what we experience. Other techniques of self-reflection, such as journaling or using a guide like the Ignatian Examen, might be helpful. Journaling obviously would not be helpful for less-literate leaders. A shortened set of oral questions might be more helpful than a written, detailed examen.

Another method of developing reflective practice, the ability to reflect on ourselves and change our attitudes and behaviors, is through peer interaction. The effectiveness of this method for continuing character development and growth in Christ was clear in early Methodism. This movement to Christ began in the mid-eighteenth century in Britain. It was organized around multitudes of small peer groups whose members held one another accountable for dealing with sin, learning the Bible, and putting what they learned into practice in daily life.

Having a similarly committed peer group and a safe space for encouraging and challenging one another helps us to be accountable for what we say we will do. Peers are usually less threatening than overseers.

Peers help one another grow and understand one another's weaknesses. Peers, as friends, are also more likely to be quick to call out inappropriate behavior. Developers should help leaders find and develop a peer group. Together they can safely help one another reflect on their attitudes and actions as disciples and leaders, and spur one another on to deeper life in Christ.

All these practices develop a habit of continual self-reflection, so self-correction can occur in real time. This is important for leaders because of their influence over others. It helps to control leaders' temptation to exploit people and resources for their own benefit.

We cannot stress enough that character is not developed through lectures or sermons. Although Scripture is the foil for reflection, we learn how it applies to daily life through people's examples. We learn from how living examples and peers apply biblical teaching in day-to-day life and ministry situations. More devotional-style talks in which people reflect on how the Bible affects their daily lives do have some value. The difference between devotional-style talks compared with lectures and sermons is their focus on experiencing God rather than transferring knowledge about the Bible. They are most effective when they make explicit the speakers' personal experiences of God.

All believers, as a fundamental of discipleship, do need to be continuing to learn the content of the Bible. But simply gaining knowledge about the Bible is not enough to transform our character. It is in living out what the Bible teaches that we grow in our faith. The power of an exemplar comes through the similarity of experience between the exemplar's experiences and our own. The more clear we can make these likenesses, especially as developers from different backgrounds, the more helpful they will be.

Humility, courage, integrity, resilience, openness, and being able to deal well with sin and failure are especially important for leaders. If we want to develop these in leaders, we first have to display them in our own lives. We bring leaders alongside us as we experience circumstances that test these qualities. We explain what we are thinking, how the Bible affects our thoughts about what we are experiencing, and how it guides how we act and self-correct our attitudes and actions. Demonstrating humility and openness includes listening to what leaders and other disciples in the context say to us, making ourselves vulnerable for the sake of their learning. This also provides an example of how they can help one another learn. We can also point out, imitate, and affirm community members who display these qualities.

As is evident in our own lives, and from the way Jesus developed his disciples, character issues are not developed through a one-off lesson. We repeatedly relearn them throughout our lives.

Complex Skills: Community, Clarity, Care

None of the skills leaders need to learn are simple. Leaders manage complex relationships in unpredictable circumstances and contexts. As people do things together, communication is critical and conflict is inevitable.

Skills are always learned best by doing. We learn from watching and copying how *people* manage people. Complex skill development is holistic in the sense that it incorporates whole people in specific contexts interacting with people.

> DEVELOP SKILLS BY DOING THEM.

Even skills which might, at first, seem simple, such as communication—if we envisage it just as the words we speak—are complex. Communication includes the physical context, nonverbal communication, and messages around the words that are not specifically spoken. It includes emotions. We cannot separate it from people's interpretations about what is going on, how different people respond, and the longer-term results of the communication. Communication skills also vary according to the purpose and style of the communication. For example, a conversation between friends differs from a formal presentation such as a sermon. A message conveyed using print or creative media, such as a flier, Facebook post, or a YouTube video also communicates. Communication must contextualize to the genre, audience, and medium of communication.

We can learn communication skills by listening to local people's evaluations of who does it well. We can ask them to explain, if possible, why they think it is good. This is important because local people will often have different opinions than us about what good communication is, based on their cultural values. Where possible, find people who do the complex skill well and get them to train, model for, and mentor leaders. We made a mistake when we wanted to train new believers in telling Bible stories. Because teenagers had been to school and were literate and available (because they didn't have the commitments of adults), we first trained teenagers to demonstrate how to tell stories. There were several disadvantages of this, not least of which being that adults did not listen to teenagers.

As the teenagers followed our example (as we trained them to do), their method of telling stories was less indigenous. This disempowered the adults because they then felt that their way was not the right way. Another disadvantage was that we had unintentionally given the teenagers status in the church which caused them to think themselves better than their elders, contrary to power-distance patterns in the culture.

We learned from this that it is better to take the extra time necessary to find the right people to demonstrate skills. Community members already recognize these people as skilled. Our role then is to empower them to develop and pass on their skills. If we had done this, we would also have learned how to tell Bible stories in a culturally fitting manner.

In a new church-planting situation skilled people may not yet be available. In this case, we recommend discovering the skills through consultation rather than just teaching what we think is best. This means gathering believers and raising a specific problem that leadership skills are needed for. Through the discussion, believers identify all the different factors contributing to the problem. As they work on its resolution, including relevant biblical insights, they identify the best approaches for dealing with the problem. This will also help to clarify what leaders' roles are in distinction to followers' roles.

Let's take the example of conflict in the church. Going through this process will help the believers to understand the important principles for biblical conflict management. It will help us, as intercultural developers, to understand how conflict is managed in the local cultural setting. If we come from low context and weak group-oriented cultures we may be unfamiliar with managing conflict using mediators or indirect means, such as meals together or gift-giving. Once we have gone through this process, we will all be more confident about the best approach for managing the problem. And we will have a clearer idea of the different skills leaders need to help resolve it.

As each skill set becomes clearer, we can develop modules to use for training in these skills. Modules are discrete training blocks. They can be used flexibly, as needed, when other leaders face the same or similar problems in their own context. Each module focuses on a problem common to leaders and the set of skills needed to deal with the problem.

Role-plays and simulations are good ways of developing these complex skills. It takes time, practice, and experience to learn how to manage self and the situation in ways that benefit rather than harm participants. A role-play is short, focusing on a single interaction. A simulation tries to recreate the whole context, including the unpredictability of how people might react in real life.

Role-plays and simulations are good ways of helping trainees *feel* what it's like to be in the situation they act. For example, conflict might evoke anger or distress, either of which may be difficult to control. Through the role-play, leaders learn how to recognize and control their emotions.

In real life, this enables them to focus on restoring relationships rather than lashing out in reaction to feelings. Experience in roles helps leaders develop and practice scripts. Scripts are helpful things to say and ways of responding which they then feel confident to use amid the chaos and emotions of real-life situations.

Role-plays and simulations should always be followed by careful and sensitive debriefing. This enables participants to safely:
(1) describe what happened
(2) explain what they felt and process their emotions
(3) analyze the dynamics from different perspectives
(4) work out helpful responses for when they encounter the same feelings and reactions in real-life situations

Follow-up discussion of these role-plays or simulations should allow for ways of giving feedback that encourage and preserve face. Learning to encourage rather than tear down is an extra skill and attitude that leaders learn through this process. Another advantage of these simulated experiences is that leaders can repeatedly practice them. This allows leaders to refine their scripts and tactics for self-control in readiness for real-life situations. Because the only resources essential for these modules are the people themselves, they are easy for leaders to reproduce to train others.

A further way of developing complex skills is through modeling and mentoring by more experienced leaders in the culture, in real life. Ideally, new leaders spend time with experienced leaders in real-life contexts. The more time together in ministry and life, the more time for experienced local leaders to influence life-to-life. If experienced local leaders are not available, the onus is on developers to model these skills.

Specific complex skill areas for leaders include:
- communication in general
- conflict management
- community decision-making
- community problem-solving
- managing specific contextual issues (like our example of the thanksgiving sacrifice)
- community articulation of vision and purpose
- building safe community
- developing community members' mutual respect and caring for one another
- empowering others
- researching the health of the church

- researching the needs of the community (inside and outside the church)
- critically engaging with the world surrounding the church

The best way to develop these is to gather context-specific examples of problems or challenges that can serve as the focus for just-in-time modular training in these areas.

5. Connect Knowledge with Experience

Most often when people develop teaching or training programs, they start with the body of knowledge that they want to transfer. For leaders, knowledge is far less important than character and skills. This does not mean that it is not important. But, rather, that it should be strictly in proportion to its importance rather than swamping everything else.

KEEP KNOWLEDGE PROPORTIONAL TO ITS RELATIVE IMPORTANCE.

It is helpful to use Ward and Rowen's idea of a two-railed fence.[1] The top rail is theory. The bottom rail is experience. The fenceposts are learning through discussion which helps to connect the two rails with each other. Plueddemann flattened the image to a railway track. This puts theory on the same level as experience with the cross-bars making connections between the two.[2] The double-headed arrows in figure 10 represent the connections between theory and experience. We make connections by reflecting on reading or through collaborative discussion. This discussion might be informal (in a meeting of peers) or formal (in a seminar).

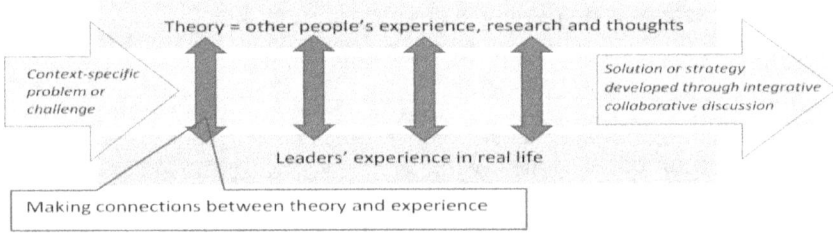

Figure 10: Making connections between life and theory

In developing leaders, ideas should never be studied for their own sake alone. They should always be examined in relation to real-life experience. The results of discussion or reflection should be applied in real life.

---

1 Ward and Rowen, "Significance of the Extension Seminary."
2 See chapter 2 in Plueddemann, *Teaching across Cultures*.

The aim is to develop a habit of asking questions which make us reflect on our experience. They prompt us to seek knowledge which might shed light on our experience. It causes us to test theory according to experience, preferably in discussion with others. It drives us to apply ideas practically.

Ideally, this becomes a continuing habit which protects the church from learning becoming isolated from everyday life. As the lead in the process is day-to-day experience, it means knowledge is continually changing as the surrounding context changes. Historical Christian truths are reaffirmed with up-to-date, relevant applications. New theologies, responsive to local contextual issues, can develop.

> BUILD A HABIT OF APPLYING KNOWLEDGE TO EVERYDAY LIFE.

Create Problem-Based, Complex Skill Training

Problem-based learning is a collaborative learning method. It is built on the belief that working together brings different perspectives to the analysis of problems and finding their solutions. Facilitating problem-based learning means that developers need to have skills in group-building, making sure that all members participate, and managing conflict. Developers also need to develop skills in managing flexible, responsive learning (because groups of people do not always follow set plans).

As group members learn to learn together, they also learn the processes of healthy group interaction, which they can then pass on to their own groups and the people they develop. As leaders become confident in this way of learning, and see how it helps them solve real-life problems, they often start applying the process to other problems they face.

These nine steps outline how to do problem-based learning.

1. **Describe the problem.** The problem can be presented by someone explaining it, watching a video, reading a case study, or eliciting it from the group. Once presented, learners retell it to make sure all essential elements have been identified and understood.
2. **Analyze the problem.** Together the group discusses the different parts of the problem, including the issues and challenges it raises.
3. **Seek out resources** to bring more understanding to the problem and its issues, along with what might help with solving it. Resources can include people, biblical and other knowledge, and skills.

4. **Make connections** between the resources and the problem. That is, work out exactly how specific resources contribute to understanding and potentially solving the problem. Often the unexpected, intuitive suggestions of some group members provide critical insights. It is important that facilitators ensure that the group does not dismiss suggestions without careful consideration of them first.

5. **Agree on solutions.** Identify what skills are needed to implement the solution. Where possible, identify skilled practitioners who can model and train the leaders in these skills.

6. **Practice the skills in the group.** This is done using role-plays or simulations, debriefing, and giving feedback that is encouraging and specific.

7. **Practice the skills in real life,** preferably with mentors. Once leaders are confident, they can try out their skills in real-life situations. They should reflect on what happens and receive feedback from experienced leaders.

8. **Reflect on personal practice.** It is good to help leaders develop a habit of personal reflection and improvement. This means they consider what they did, their attitudes, peoples' responses, and how they can improve next time.

9. **Pass it on.** Not only is "passing it on" the 2 Timothy 2:2 principle, it also benefits learners. In the passing on, they learn more deeply. They learn from the collaborative process of problem-based learning itself. They also learn the specifics of the different skills.

The good thing about a problem-based approach is that it can be built up gradually, in response to real-life problems as they occur. It provides leaders with experience in a process that they can use to solve problems in the future. Once there is a library of modules, these can be used just-in-time as developers visit leaders in different ministry contexts. Leaders can also use them with peers or new leaders.

The basic ingredients of problem-based learning are a problem and a process. With time, developers will have gathered a library of problems (written or oral). As many groups go through the process, developers become familiar with the best ways to resolve the problems in their context. They also become more familiar with which Bible passages are most relevant, or which resources from outside (such as examples from Christian history) are most useful to consider. This helps with facilitating discussion in new groups.

In the book's final chapter we describe three common leadership-development contexts and consider how the leadership-development principles apply in each.

> EMPOWER LEADERS TO SOLVE COMPLEX PROBLEMS
> BY USING A CONSISTENT PROCESS.

CHAPTER 14

Putting Leadership-Development into Practice

Each situation in which developers work is different. In this final chapter, we explain what leadership development could look like in three types of context that developers commonly find themselves in. We assume that developers know the language and have a good understanding of the leaders' culture. First we describe the context, then how we would develop leaders in that setting using the five principles outlined in chapter 13.

Context 1—Pioneer Church Planting

The first context is "pioneer church planting," in a region where there are no other churches made up of members of this people group. The church is very small. Most church participants are poor or have been marginalized by their own people group (e.g., they had already rejected the dominant religion). They may be dependent on the church planters for support (material or emotional), or are teenagers or children.

An example of this is a group of young men in a Muslim-majority country. Although they are from a Muslim background, before they became disciples of Jesus they had already rejected Islam. Some had been atheists and stopped taking part in Islamic activities. The church planters have had no contact with these young men's families. No attendee of the regular meeting is a natural leader by community standards. Their faith is precarious. If the church planters had to leave, it is unclear whether the church would continue.

At this stage of the church-planting effort, it is too early to be considering leadership development. Church members could be encouraged to take on responsibility. But the focus of the church planters should be on discipling. The disciplers' major focus should be on family relationships. Without this, the church will not embed in the community and Christians will become isolated from the wider community.

If the church planters unexpectedly have to leave because of visa issues, political conflict, or health concerns, this could actually work out for the good. Then members who have leadership gifting may emerge to lead the group. If the church planters return, it is important for them to support the leaders who have emerged. This is the case even if they don't look like leaders in the church planters' home churches. The church planters should resist taking back responsibility.

Leadership development then becomes a collaborative process of growing the church together. As issues arise, the church planters and local leaders can engage in a contextualization discussion together, further developing both sides' understanding of how the Bible applies to the local context.

Summary of Applying the Leadership-Development Principles

1. Church members all need to be discipled together, growing as a community.
2. Until leaders naturally emerge, it could be harmful to the church to separate out some for "special" leadership development.
3. Involve the whole church in working out what culturally fitting leadership and accountability should look like.
4./5. The church planters' focus will be on developing the maturity of all believers individually and together as a group. It is too soon for specific leaders' complex skill development. If issues come up in the group, the whole group can consult together to find biblical and culturally fitting solutions. Once they agree together on how to manage issues well, they then put it into practice (e.g., conflict in the group; accountability for group money). This gives developers the extra advantage of seeing who has influence in the group. The whole group learns how to apply the Bible to everyday life.

Context 2—Movement of Multiplying Churches

The second context is a movement where small churches are multiplying over a large geographical area. Developers have experience in leading churches in this movement. Because of the rapid growth, there has been very little discipling. Most people do not or cannot read. The Bible is not available in a written form that most people understand. Leaders have emerged from within the churches, but they are as undiscipled as other church members.

It is particularly important in this case for developers to respect and honor the existing leaders rather than judge them for poor standards of Christian living. Instead of jumping straight in to develop the leaders, the first work is to strengthen discipling across the whole church. This should empower all disciples, including leaders, to disciple themselves and new believers. Increasing the churches' general understanding of biblical teaching and standards helps the whole church to establish a foundation of what it means to be Christians in their cultural context. This also provides a foundation to determine what an exemplary Christian disciple looks like, and therefore what Christian leaders should look like.

When developers judge existing leaders as substandard, it can be tempting to ignore them and select young, more malleable people to develop as leaders instead. Not only does this undermine and dishonor existing leaders, it will probably result in severe frustration for those young people, or split churches. Established leaders often see the younger people as immature, disrespectful, and impatient when they push for change according to what they have learned from outsiders.

It is better to work with the leaders who exist rather than provoking conflict and division. Remember that these are God's people and God's church. Our role is to build it up, not tear it apart. It is worth taking the time to build relationships with existing leaders, see them in context, and learn about how they do leadership. We can explore with them, and the whole church, how their Christian leadership compares with leadership in the surrounding non-Christian community. It may also be helpful to discuss how it compares with leadership in close-by cultural groups with established churches. These discussions should generate many specific examples of what Christian leadership among this cultural group looks like. They should also clarify what followers can expect and how they can support their leaders.

Over time, developers should be gathering a bank of examples of typical problems, issues, challenges, and complex incidents that can be used for specific complex-skill training. These examples can first be used to develop pilot-training modules. Pilot-training modules can be trialed with different groups of leaders and followers. Through this, developers can improve them so leaders can easily understand the issues and what to do. With the passing of time, developers create a library of contextually relevant, problem-based modules. Developers can easily use them when visiting churches or when groups of leaders come together for seminars or conferences. As the modules start with familiar incidents and are self-contained, they are also more easily reproduced by the leaders as they develop new and emerging leaders in their own churches.

Developers should also work with the churches to set up culturally fitting systems that protect leaders and followers from leaders' vulnerabilities. We cannot protect leaders from vulnerability just by teaching them about it. We have to work with churches to set up accountability for leaders in locally sustainable ways. Churches that prove to have good processes can become resources to help other churches. Seminars which gather people from across the movement are often a good way of fostering sharing experience between different churches.

As developers working across multiple churches, we should also be continuously aware of the need to reproduce ourselves. Then leadership development can reproduce itself without us. Intentionally building a repeating DNA into the way we do things means that it can spread more easily to churches beyond our geographical reach and continue if we have to leave.

Summary of Applying the Leadership-Development Principles

1. Developers need to work on developing discipleship across the whole church, including leaders alongside all disciples.
2. Select leaders for development who are already leading. This includes small-group leaders as well as pastors of larger churches.
3. Work with the whole church to discover what leadership and accountability should look like. Invest time in helping churches set up healthy support and accountability structures for leaders.
4. Specific leadership development is appropriate because there are already leaders in place (in contrast to Context 1). Developers should, whenever possible, spend time with leaders in their groups. Through building relationships with leaders and their communities, developers will be more able to model attitudes, behaviors, self-reflection, and complex skills. Time with communities, or perhaps with groups of leaders in seminars, provides opportunities to note issues, gather examples, and do specific training in complex skills. This enables developers to create problem-based modules to use flexibly in different settings.
5. With time, developers create a library of complex skill-training modules based on the practical experience of leaders. Developers can use the modules individually or combine them for longer development events (e.g., half-day or daylong workshops, or

weeklong seminars). Through the process of problem-solving, leaders gain experience in connecting biblical and other theory with life in a practical way. Problem-based learning gives the leaders a process they can use to solve other problems they face. If they use it with their communities, the whole group develops as a reflective community.

Context 3—Churches in Contexts Where Pastors Are Expected to Attend Bible Colleges

Perhaps the most difficult context is where Bible colleges already exist. This can occur even in new church-planting situations. Often, missionaries set up colleges early in the life of the church. This causes much pressure for the pattern of leadership, and leadership development, to conform to the institutional pattern. However, easily reproducible, problem-based, modular leadership development is still possible. Developers who are alongside leaders in their churches can flexibly develop leaders in parallel to the college programs. It may be possible to propose that specific modules be included in college programs for practical learning.

It is very difficult to overcome the influence of the institutional approach. Degrees confer status. Most denominations require degrees for ordination. It is better to accept this reality than to burn out trying to overcome it. Work out how to work with the system rather than in opposition to it.

For leaders who do not naturally fit the institutional pattern, we may need to negotiate pathways and support for them. Otherwise they will not be successful in the institutions. Without this, the needs of indigenous and minority-group leaders are unlikely to be met. The wider church will not hear their voices. The global church will not learn from them about what it means to follow Jesus.

This will hinder developing an indigenous church in an unreached people group. It also suppresses minority churches, as their leaders are forced into the dominant people group's leadership mold. In the post-Christian West, the dominant church misses out on learning from the insights of growing migrant churches.

Summary of Applying the Leadership-Development Principles

1. It is likely that others will already be working on discipleship programs in the churches. This means that developers do not need to develop discipleship across the churches. For discipling,

therefore, developers rely on others discipling leaders. Their focus is on selection processes which ensure that leaders are being well discipled. Without a focus on careful selection, leadership development often becomes remedial discipleship.

2. As the colleges will be viewed as the best training for pastors, developers should focus on the less visible leaders in churches. They are less likely to attend Bible colleges. But they will still be leading and endorsed by their communities.

3. If the church already has denominational structures, there will already be institutional expectations around leader accountability. However, there may be groups within a church who are not from the majority group (e.g., a Kurdish group within a German church in Germany). These groups may be allowed to set up their own indigenous structures and community life. It could be helpful to give intercultural training to leaders from minorities to help them manage dominant group expectations. The developer has to find a balance between nurturing life in its fullness within the minority-culture group while acting as a mediator between minority and majority leaders. A specific incident related to the challenge of intercultural interaction would be a good basis for a problem-based learning module that benefits both minority-group leaders and majority-group leaders.

4. There is still a place for developing the 4 Cs alongside leaders in their communities. In the same way, developing understanding of complex skills together with community members could be very helpful. Especially if the complex-skill training is easily reproducible, it has the potential to help many leaders across the churches.

    Easily reproducible, problem-based, complex-skill focused training modules could be a valuable resource for pastors learning in Bible colleges. They could then use them when they move into their churches. These could help pastors develop important skills, as well as pass them on to others.

5. All leaders, including pastors, who do problem-based learning and apply it in ministry, learn how to connect knowledge with everyday experience. They grow in applying theory to practical life. The more experience they have in the problem-based learning process, the more it will help them develop a habit of reflection on practice.

Do Life with Leaders

We multiply leaders by doing life with them, walking alongside them in their communities. Just as leaders become examples for their followers, developers are examples for leaders. We model Christlike character, how to strengthen the community as it fulfills its purpose, including how to empower members of the community to flourish together, use their God-given gifts, and care for one another. The more we are in the community with leaders, the more we can model encouragement, inclusivity, and humility. We too are simply believers, the same as every other follower of Christ.

Leaders, like all disciples, need to grow in biblical understanding and the ability to apply the Bible to everyday life. As leaders have to be able to teach others, we can help them (and all believers) by modeling teaching that is easily reproducible in the local context. We, ourselves, can learn how to teach from gifted local teachers, and promote leaders learning from them also.

Christian leaders are Jesus's disciples who have followers. If we spend time in their communities, we should be able to identify leaders by first identifying their groups. Even when we think we have identified leaders, it is always best to confirm this with their community. The people who leaders live and work with will be best able to evaluate how mature they are as disciples and how well they are growing in Christlike character and community-building. Our natural tendency to view things from our own cultural perspective can make us less able to evaluate leaders' attitudes and behaviors according to culturally expressed biblical standards.

Developing leaders also means developing the communities they belong to. It is good for us, as developers, to watch and learn how group members in the culture work together and make decisions. We can encourage leaders, together with their communities, to search the Scriptures to find biblical insights they can apply to local issues. In this way, developers enable the group to make decisions that honor and respect the Bible. They also learn how to evaluate their culture in the light of Scripture. As they discuss and work together, they also learn to value the gifts and contribution of each group member. We have done our job well if the community, along with its leaders, can develop and multiply without us.

Our purpose as developers is to empower leaders to transform the groups they lead into all that God wants them to be. These leaders have much to teach us. As we learn, with them, what it means for Jesus to be at home in the many cultural contexts of this world, we together, build up the church, the body of Christ … [so that we all] will be mature in the Lord, measuring up to the full and complete standard of Christ … so that the whole body is healthy and growing and full of love. (Eph 4:12–13, 16)

> EMPOWER THE COMMUNITY AND ITS LEADERS TO DEVELOP AND MULTIPLY WITHOUT YOU.

Acknowledgments

It was emotionally difficult to give myself to writing this book after Richard's death. My daughter, Ümit Kennedy, has been a great support. Her encouragement helped me to keep writing. She reviewed the first of several drafts of this book, and different sections thereafter. She did this while managing the demands of two small children during several COVID isolations. Her emotional, practical, and consistent support is of immeasurable value.

A number of people who knew Richard also contributed by reviewing the second draft. Their insightful comments and detailed feedback improved the book significantly. I am grateful to Aaron Koh, Barbara Williamson, Carolyn and Jerry Moyer, Julyan Lidstone, Ross and Lyndal Webb, and another couple who work in a country for which it is better not to publish their names. All these reviewers have extensive experience in intercultural ministry and have helped ground the book in practical reality.

I also acknowledge the many people Richard interviewed and whose experiences informed this book.

Many leaders from the Millet and other cultures gave us insights about effective leadership and its development in different cultural settings. It has been a great privilege to walk alongside them.

The women of the Angelina Noble Centre (ANC) have stood by me in my grief and through a crisis of institutional belonging for the ANC. Their presence and generous ministry to others constantly reminds me of unrecognized leaders firmly embedded in nurturing community.

About the Authors

Evelyn and Richard Hibbert were pioneer church planters among Turkish speakers in Bulgaria. During that time, they also developed leadership training for a movement of thousands of Muslim-background believers to Christ. They have since taught cross-cultural missions and education, and advised missionaries serving across the world. Richard was the Director of the Centre for Cross-Cultural Mission at the Sydney Missionary and Bible College in Australia up until his death from cancer in 2020. Evelyn is the leader of the Angelina Noble Centre, a research center for women involved in cross-cultural mission.

Bibliography

Adeyemo, Tokunbeh. "Servant Leadership in an African Context." *AIM Magazine* (August 1998): 3–4.

Aktas, M., M. J. Gelfand, and P. J. Hanges. "Cultural Tightness–Looseness and Perceptions of Effective Leadership." *Journal of Cross-Cultural Psychology* 47, no. 2 (2016): 294–309.

Ao, Louis, and David Penley. *Cross-Cultural Leadership: Ministering to a Multicultural Community*. Xulon Press, 2006.

Aycan, Zeynep. "Cross-Cultural Approaches to Leadership." Chap. 13 in *The Handbook of Cross-Cultural Management Research*, edited by Peter Bevington Smith, Mark F. Peterson, and David C. Thomas, 219–238. Los Angeles: Sage, 2008.

Aycan, Zeynep, Birgit Schyns, Jian-Min Sun, Jörg Felfe, and Noreen Saher. "Convergence and Divergence of Paternalistic Leadership: A Cross-Cultural Investigation of Prototypes." *Journal of International Business Studies* 44, no. 9 (2013): 962–69.

Banks, Robert, and Bernice M. Ledbetter. *Reviewing Leadership: A Christian Evaluation of Current Approaches*. Engaging Culture. Grand Rapids: Baker Academic, 2004.

Bass, Bernard M., and Ruth Bass. *The Bass Handbook of Leadership: Theory, Research, and Managerial Applications*. 4th ed. New York: Free Press, 2008.

Bennett, David. "The Leader As … Friend … Brother/Sister … Servant … ." *Transformation*, no. 13, no. 1 (1996): 12–19.

Brodbeck, Felix C., Jagdeep Singh Chhokar, and Robert J. House. "Culture and Leadership in 25 Societies: Integration, Conclusions, and Future Directions." In *Culture and Leadership across the World: The GLOBE Book of In-Depth Studies of 25 Societies*, edited by Jagdeep Singh Chhokar, Felix C. Brodbeck and Robert J. House, 1023–84. Mahwah, NJ: Lawrence Erlbaum Associates, 2007.

Brynjolfson, Robert, and Jonathan Lewis, eds. *Integral Ministry Training: Design and Evaluation*. Pasadena: William Carey Library, 2006.

Burke, David, Richard Brown, and Julius Qaiser, eds. *TEE for the 21st Century*. Carlisle, UK: Langham Publishing, 2021.

Burns, James MacGregor. *Leadership*. 1st ed. New York: Harper & Row, 1978.

Calhoun, Adele Ahlberg. *Spiritual Disciplines Handbook: Practices That Transform Us*. Downers Grove: IVP Books, 2015.

Carey, Freda, and Patricia Harrison. "TEE in Historical Context." Chap. 4 in *TEE for the 21st Century*, edited by David Burke, Richard Brown, and Julius Qaiser, 92–111. Carlisle, UK: Langham Publishing, 2021.

Chang, Peter. "Steak, Potatoes, Peas and Chopsuey: Linear and Non-Linear Thinking." In *Missions and Theological Education in World Perspective*, edited by Harvie Conn and Samuel F. Rowen, 113–23. Farmington, MI: Associates of Urbanus, 1984.

Chhokar, Jagdeep Singh, Felix C. Brodbeck, Robert J. House, and Global Leadership and Organizational Behavior Effectiveness Research Program. *Culture and Leadership across the World: The GLOBE Book of In-Depth Studies of 25 Societies.* Mahwah, NJ: Lawrence Erlbaum Associates, 2007.

Chiang, Samuel, and Grant Lovejoy, eds. *Beyond Literate Western Contexts: Honor & Shame and Assessment of Orality Preference.* Hong Kong: International Orality Network, 2015.

Chinchen, Del. "The Patron-Client System: A Model of Indigenous Discipleship." *Evangelical Missions Quarterly* 31, no. 4 (1994): 446–451.

Chrispal, Ashish. "Restoring Missional Vision in Theological Education: The Need for Transformative Pastoral Training in the Majority World." *Lausanne Global Analysis* 8, no. 5 (2019).

Corwin, Gary. "Leadership as Pain-Bearing." *Evangelical Missions Quarterly* 34, no. 1 (1998): 16–17.

Corwin, Gary. "The Multi-Tasking Challenge of Training for Church Leadership." *Evangelical Missions Quarterly* 43, no. 2 (2007): 144–145.

David, D. R. "India Leadership Study: A Summary for Christian Leaders." (2002). http://www.firstfruit.org/india-leadership-study.

Dickson, Marcus W., Deanne N. Den Hartog, and Jacqueline K. Mitchelson. 2003. "Research on Leadership in a Cross-Cultural Context: Making Progress, and Raising New Questions." *The Leadership Quarterly* 14: 729–768.

Earley, P. C. "Social Loafing and Collectivism." *Administrative Science Quarterly* 34, no. 4 (1989): 565–81.

Elashmawi, Farid, and Philip R. Harris. *Multicultural Management: New Skills for Global Success.* Managing Cultural Differences Series. Houston: Gulf Pub., 1993.

Elliston, Edgar J. *Home Grown Leaders.* Pasadena, CA: William Carey Library, 1992.

Elliston, Edgar J., and J. Timothy Kauffman. *Developing Leaders for Urban Ministries.* American University Studies Series VII, Theology and Religion. New York: P. Lang, 1993.

Elmer, Duane. *Cross-Cultural Conflict: Building Relationships for Effective Ministry.* Downers Grove: InterVarsity Press, 1993.

Eyong, J. E. "Indigenous African Leadership: Key Differences from Anglo-Centric Thinking and Writings." *Leadership* 13, no. 2 (2017): 133–53.

Ferris, Robert, ed. *Establishing Ministry Training: A Manual for Program Developers.* Pasadena, CA: William Carey Library, 1995.

Fields, M. "Hundreds of Churches in Honduras." n.d.

Flanders, Christopher. "Honor and Shame: A Review of the Process and Articles." In *Beyond Literate Western Contexts: Honor & Shame and Assessment of Orality Preference,* edited by Samuel Chiang and Grant Lovejoy, 77–90. Hong Kong: International Orality Network, 2015.

Fordjor, Peter, Agnes Kotoh, Kwame Kumah Kpeli, Albert Kwamefio, Quarm Bernard Mensa, Esther Owusu, and Barbara Mullins. "A Review of Traditional Ghanaian and Western Philosophies of Adult Education." *International Journal of Lifelong Education* 22, no. 2 (2003): 182–99.

Franklin, Kirk. "Culture Does Affect Our Spirituality." In *Spirituality in Mission: Embracing the Lifelong Journey*, edited by John Amalraj, Geoffrey Hahn, and William Taylor, loc 2549–709, Kindle. Pasadena, CA: William Carey Library, 2018.

Fu, P. P., R. Wu, and Y. Yang. "Chinese Culture and Leadership." In *Culture and Leadership across the World: The GLOBE Book of In-Depth Studies of 25 Societies*, edited by Jagdeep Singh Chhokar, Felix C. Brodbeck, and Robert J. House, 877–907. Mahwah, NJ: Lawrence Erlbaum Associates, 2007.

Fulton, Brent. "Beyond Theological Education." *ChinaSource* (2016). Published electronically March 2. https://www.chinasource.org/resource-library/blog-entries/beyond-theological-education.

Georges, Jayson. *Ministering in Patronage Cultures: Biblical Models and Missional Implications*. Downers Grove: InterVarsity Press, 2019.

Gitau, Wanjiru. "Formation of African Christian Leaders: Patterns from the ALS Data." In *African Christian Leadership: Realities, Opportunities, and Impact*, edited by Robert J. Priest and A. Kirimi Barine, 1320–7848, Kindle. Maryknoll, NY: Orbis Books, 2017.

Graham, Robert. "The Role of Perception of Time in Consumer Research." *Journal of Consumer Research* 7, no. 4 (1981): 335–42.

Greenlee, David, and James Stuck. "Individualist Educators in a Collectivist Society: Insights from a Cross-Cultural Model Applied to China." *Missiology: An International Review* 32, no. 4 (2004): 491–504.

Gupta, Vipin, and Montgomery Van Wart. *Leadership across the Globe*. New York: Routledge, 2016.

Haire, Mason. "Biological Models and Empirical History of the Growth of Organizations." In *Modern Organization Theory: A Symposium of the Foundation for Research on Human Behavior*, edited by Mason Haire, 272–306. New York: Garland Pub., 1959.

Hall, Edward T. *The Silent Language*. 1st ed. Garden City, NY: Doubleday, 1959.

Heath, Shirley Brice. *Ways with Words: Language, Life, and Work in Communities and Classrooms*. New York: Cambridge University Press, 1983.

Hibbert, Evelyn, and Richard Yates Hibbert. *Training Missionaries: Principles and Possibilities*. Pasadena, CA: William Carey Library, 2016.

Hibbert, Evelyn, and Richard Yates Hibbert. *Walking Together on the Jesus Road: Discipling in Intercultural Contexts*. Littleton, CO: William Carey Publishing, 2018.

Hibbert, Richard Yates. "Why Do They Leave? An Ethnographic Investigation of Defection from Turkish-Speaking Roma Churches in Bulgaria." *Missiology: An International Review* 41, no. 3 (2013): 315–28.

Hibbert, Richard Yates, and Evelyn Hibbert. "Defining Culturally Appropriate Leadership." *Missiology: An International Review* 47, no. 3 (2019): 240–51.

Hibbert, Richard Yates, and Evelyn Hibbert. "Diagnosing Church Health across Cultures: A Case Study of Turkish Gypsy Churches in Bulgaria." *Missiology: An International Review* 44, no. 3 (2016): 243–56.

Hibbert, Richard Yates, and Evelyn Hibbert. "Managing Conflict in a Multicultural Team." *Evangelical Missions Quarterly* 53, no. 3 (2017): 18–23.

Hiebert, Paul G. *Anthropological Insights for Missionaries.* Grand Rapids: Baker, 1985.

Hiebert, Paul G. *Transforming Worldviews: An Anthropological Understanding of How People Change.* Grand Rapids: Baker Academic, 2008.

Hodges, Melvin L. *The Indigenous Church; Including the Indigenous Church and the Missionary.* Rev. ed. Springfield, MO: Gospel Publishing House, 2009.

Hofstede, Geert. https://geerthofstede.com/culture-geert-hofstede-gert-jan-hofstede/6d-model-of-national-culture/.

Hofstede, Geert H., Gert Jan Hofstede, and Michael Minkov. *Cultures and Organizations: Software of the Mind: Intercultural Cooperation and Its Importance for Survival.* 3rd ed. New York: McGraw-Hill, 2010.

Hoppe, M. H. "Cross-Cultural Issues in the Development of Leaders." In *The Center for Creative Leadership Handbook of Leadership Development*, edited by Cynthia D. McCauley and Ellen Van Velsor, 331–60. San Francisco: Jossey-Bass, 2004.

House, R. J., N. Wright, and R. N. Aditya. "Cross-Cultural Research on Organizational Leadership: A Critical Analysis and a Proposed Theory." In *New Perspectives on International Industrial/Organizational Psychology*, edited by C. Earley and M. Erez, 535–625. San Francisco: The New Lexington Press, 1997.

House, Robert J. *Strategic Leadership across Cultures: The GLOBE Study of CEO Leadership Behavior and Effectiveness in 24 Countries.* Thousand Oaks, CA: SAGE Publications, Inc., 2014.

House, Robert J., Paul J. Hanges, Mansour Javidan, Peter W. Dorfman, and Vipin Gupta. *Culture, Leadership, and Organizations: The GLOBE Study of 62 Societies.* Thousand Oaks, CA.: Sage Publications, 2004.

Hunter, Ross. "Discipleship Training: A Non-Traditional Approach to Theological Education for the Highland Quichua of Ecuador." *Evangelical Missions Quarterly* 54, no. 2 (2018): 40–45.

ICETE. "Manifesto on the Renewal of Evangelical Theological Education." International Council for Evangelical Theological Education, http://www.icete-edu.org/manifesto/.

Jackson, T. H. *International HRM: A Cross-Cultural Approach.* Thousand Oaks, CA: SAGE, 2002.

Jackson, Terence. "Paternalistic Leadership." *International Journal of Cross Cultural Management* 16, no. 1 (2016): 3–7.

"Japanese Employer Explains Lunchbreak Punishment on TV." *The Guardian*, June 22, 2018.

Johnson, David, and Jeffrey VanVonderen. *The Subtle Power of Spiritual Abuse*. Minneapolis: Bethany House Publishers, 1991.

Johnson, Jean. *We Are Not the Hero: A Missionary's Guide to Sharing Christ, Not a Culture of Dependency*. Sisters, OR: Deep River Books, 2016.

Karsten, N., and F. Hendriks. "Don't Call Me a Leader, but I Am One: The Dutch Mayor and the Tradition of Bridging-and-Bonding Leadership in Consensus Democracies." *Leadership* 13, no. 2 (2017): 154–72.

Khan, A., J. Zolkiewski, and J. Murphy. "Favour and Opportunity: Renqing in Chinese Business Relationships." *Journal of Business and Industrial Marketing* 31, no. 2 (2016): 183–92.

Koeshall, Anita. "Navigating Power–Liquid Power Structures for Molten Times." In *Devoted to Christ*, edited by Christopher Flanders. Eugene, OR: Pickwick Publications, 2019.

Lausanne Movement. "The Cape Town Commitment." Lausanne Movement, https://www.lausanne.org/content/ctc/ctcommitment.

Lee, Sunghee, Mingnan Liu, and Mengyao Hu. "Relationship between Future Time Orientation and Item Nonresponse on Subject Probability Questions: A Cross-Cultural Analysis." *Journal of Cross-Cultural Psychology* 48, no. 5 (2017): 698–717.

Lencioni, Patrick. *The Five Dysfunctions of a Team: A Leadership Fable*. San Francisco: Jossey-Bass, 2002.

Lidstone, Julyan. *Give Up the Purple: A Call for Servant Leadership in Hierarchical Cultures*. Carlisle, UK: Langham Global Library, 2019.

Lingenfelter, Judith, and Sherwood G. Lingenfelter. *Teaching Cross-Culturally: An Incarnational Model for Learning and Teaching*. Grand Rapids: Baker Academic, 2003.

Lingenfelter, Sherwood G. *Leading Cross-Culturally: Covenant Relationships for Effective Christian Leadership*. Grand Rapids: Baker Academic, 2008.

Livermore, David A. *Serving with Eyes Wide Open: Doing Short-Term Missions with Cultural Intelligence*. Grand Rapids: Baker Books, 2006.

Madinger, Charles. "Will Our Message 'Stick'? Assessing a Dominant Preference for Orality for Education and Training." In *Beyond Literate Western Contexts: Honor & Shame and Assessment of Orality Preference*, edited by Samuel Chiang and Grant Lovejoy, 125–34. Hong Kong: International Orality Network, 2015.

Malunga, Chiku. "Learning Leadership Development from African Cultures: A Personal Perspective." *INTRC Praxis Note* 25 (2006). https://sarpn.org/documents/d0002248/African_cultures_Malunga_Sept2006.pdf.

Mandryk, Jason. *Operation World: The Definitive Prayer Guide to Every Nation*. 7th ed. Downers Grove: InterVarsity Press, 2010.

Matsumoto, D. *Culture and Psychology: People around the World.* 2nd ed. London: Wadsworth, 2000.

Mbiti, John S. *African Religions and Philosophy.* Heinemann, 1969.

McConnell, Douglas. *Cultural Insights for Christian Leaders: New Directions for Organizations Serving God's Mission.* Mission in Global Community. Grand Rapids: Baker Academic, 2018.

Mehn, John. "What Kind of Leaders Reproduce Churches?" *Evangelical Missions Quarterly* 52, no. 2 (2016): 180–88.

Meyer, Erin. *The Culture Map: Breaking through the Invisible Boundaries of Global Business.* New York: PublicAffairs, 2014.

Mittal, R., and S. M. Elias. "Social Power and Leadership in Cross-Cultural Context." *Journal of Management Development* 35, no. 2 (2016): 58–74.

Moberg, David O. *The Church as a Social Institution: The Sociology of American Religion.* 2nd ed. Grand Rapids: Baker Book House, 1984.

Moreau, A. Scott. "A Critique of John Mbiti's Understanding of the African Concept of Time." *East African Journal of Evangelical Theology* 5, no. 2 (1986): 36–48.

Muir, Elizabeth Gillan. *A Women's History of the Christian Church: Two Thousand Years of Female Leadership.* Ontario, Canada: University of Toronto Press, 2019.

Mutabazi, Evalde. "Preparing African Leaders." In *Cross-Cultural Approaches to Leadership Development*, edited by C. Brooklyn Derr, Sylvie Roussillon, and Frank Bournois, 202–23. Westport, CT: Quorum Books, 2002.

Nah, Yoonkyeong. "Can a Self-Directed Learner Be Independent, Autonomous and Interdependent?: Implications for Practice." *Adult Learning* 11, no. 1 (1999).

Ngaruiya, David K. "Characteristics of Influential African Leaders." In *African Christian Leadership: Realities, Opportunities, and Impact*, edited by Robert J. Priest and A. Kirimi Barine, 855–1284, Kindle. Maryknoll, NY: Orbis Books, 2017.

Nouwen, Henri J. M. *In the Name of Jesus: Reflections on Christian Leadership.* New York: Crossroad, 1989.

Ortiz, Michael A. "Lessons from TEE That Invite ICETE Reflection." Chap. 21 in *TEE for the 21st Century*, edited by David Burke, Richard Brown, and Julius Qaiser, 392–98. Carlisle, UK: Langham Publishing, 2021.

Ortner, Sherry B. *Anthropology and Social Theory: Culture, Power, and the Acting Subject.* Durham, NC: Duke University Press, 2006.

Ott, Bernhard. *Understanding and Developing Theological Education.* Kindle ed. Carlisle, UK: Langham Global Library, 2016.

Ott, Craig. *Teaching and Learning across Cultures: A Guide to Theory and Practice.* Grand Rapids: Baker Academic, 2021.

Overstreet, Jane. *Unleader: The Surprising Qualities of a Valuable Leader.* Downers Grove: InterVarsity Press, 2012.

Pellegrini, Ekin, and Terri Scandura. "Paternalistic Leadership: A Review and Agenda for Future Research." *Academy of Management Annual Proceedings* 34, no. 3 (2007): 566–93.

Phillips, David J. *Peoples on the Move: Introducing Nomads of the World.* Pasadena, CA: William Carey Library, 2001.

Pithers, R. T. "Cognitive Learning Style: A Review of the Field Dependent-Field Independent Approach." *Journal of Vocational Education and Training* 54, no. 1 (2002).

Plueddemann, Jim. *Leading across Cultures: Effective Ministry and Mission in the Global Church.* Downers Grove: IVP Academic, 2012.

Plueddemann, Jim. *Teaching across Cultures: Contextualizing Education for Global Mission.* Downers Grove: InterVarsity Press, 2018.

Robert, Dana L. "World Christianity as a Women's Movement." *International Bulletin of Mission Research* 30, no. 4 (2006).

Sanneh, Lamin O. *Translating the Message: The Missionary Impact on Culture.* American Society of Missiology Series. Maryknoll, NY: Orbis Books, 1989.

Schreiter, Robert J. *The New Catholicity: Theology between the Global and the Local.* Faith and Cultures Series. Maryknoll, NY: Orbis Books, 1997.

Seaton, Ash. "Lunch with Ash." In *Forged on the Field: Letters from Mission Leaders*, 403–38. Llanwit Major: Peregrini Press, 2015.

Shaw, Perry. *Transforming Theological Education: A Practical Handbook for Integrative Learning.* Carlisle, UK: Langham Publishing, 2014.

Shaw, Perry, Cesar Lopes, Joanna Feliciano-Soberano, and Bob Heaton, eds. *Teaching across Cultures: A Global Christian Perspective*, ICETE. Carlisle, UK: Langham Global Library, 2021.

Shellnutt, Kate. "Willow Creek Investigation: Allegations against Bill Hybels Are Credible." *Christianity Today* (2019). Published electronically February 28. https://www.christianitytoday.com/news/2019/february/willow-creek-bill-hybels-investigation-iag-report.html.

Steers, R. M., C. Sanchez-Runde, and L. Nardon. "Leadership in a Global Context: New Directions in Research and Theory Development." *Journal of World Business* 47, no. 4 (2012): 479–82.

Swailes, Stephen, and Barbara Senior. "Belbin's Team Role Model: Development, Validity and Applications for Team Building." *Journal of Management Studies* 44, no. 1 (2007): 96–118.

Thomas, Gary. *Sacred Pathways: Discover Your Soul's Path to God.* Grand Rapids: Zondervan, 2000.

Tutu, Desmond. *God Has a Dream: A Vision of Hope for Our Time.* New York: Image Books, 2005.

Van Velsor, Ellen, and Cynthia D. McCauley. "Introduction: Our View of Leadership Development." Chap. 1 in *The Center for Creative Leadership Handbook of Leadership Development*, edited by Cynthia D. McCauley and Ellen Van Velsor, 1–22. San Francisco: Jossey-Bass, 2003.

Vella, Jane Kathryn. *Learning to Listen, Learning to Teach: The Power of Dialogue in Educating Adults.* The Jossey-Bass Higher and Adult Education Series. Rev. ed. San Francisco: Jossey-Bass, 2002.

Walls, Andrew F. *The Missionary Movement in Christian History: Studies in the Transmission of Faith.* Maryknoll, NY: Orbis Books, 1996.

Ward, Ted W. "Servants, Leaders, and Tyrants." In *Missions and Theological Education in World Perspective*, edited by Harvie M. Conn and Samuel F. Rowen, 19–40. Farmington: Associates of Urbanus, 1984.

Ward, Ted Warren, and Samuel F. Rowen. "The Significance of the Extension Seminary." *Evangelical Missions Quarterly* 8, no. 4 (1972): 17–27.

Watkins, David. "Learning and Teaching: A Cross-Cultural Perspective." *School Leadership and Management* 20, no. 2 (2000): 161–73.

Wesseling, J. "Culturally Conceived Systems for Healthy Groups: Western and Eastern Paradigms in Contrast." *Evangelical Missions Quarterly* 53, no. 3 (2017): 18–23.

Willard, Dallas. *Renovation of the Heart: Putting on the Character of Christ.* Colorado Springs: NavPress, 2002.

"Women in World Christianity." Center for the Study of Global Christianity, Gordon Conwell Theological Seminary, https://www.gordonconwell.edu/center-for-global-christianity/research/women-in-world-christianity/.

Zimbardo, Philip, and John Boyd. "Putting Time in Perspective: A Valid, Reliable Individual-Differences Metric." *Journal of Personality and Social Psychology* 77, no. 6 (1999): 1271–88.

More Books by Evelyn & Richard Hibbert

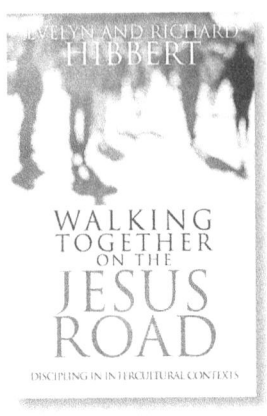

Walking Together on the Jesus Road: Discipling in Intercultural Contexts | Paperback & ePub

Walking Together on the Jesus Road guides readers through three essential practices for making disciples across cultures: listening to disciples to get to know them and their context, focusing on relationships with Christ, fellow disciples, and others, and enabling disciples to live out their faith in culturally relevant ways. The book also engages with practical challenges, such as enabling disciples to find and belong to a nurturing community of faith, as well as contextualizing the way we teach the Bible.

Leading Multicultural Teams | Paperback & ePub

This book integrates insights from the Bible, team theory, leadership, and intercultural studies to explain how leaders of multicultural teams can help their teams become enriching and enjoyable contexts to work in, at the same time as achieving their purpose. Team leaders need to know how to help team members grow in particular qualities and acquire specific skills related to multicultural teamwork.

Training Missionaries: Principals and Possibilities | Paperback & ePub

Effective training has been shown to prevent people from prematurely leaving the field. It also reduces the danger of cross-cultural workers uncritically exporting culturally bound forms of Christianity. This book details four key areas that every missionary training program, whatever its context, must focus on developing. It shows how these can be holistically addressed in a learning community where trainers and trainees engage in cross-cultural ministry together.

Available at missionbooks.com

Other Leadership Books You May Enjoy

Learning to Lead at the Feet of Jesus
Todd Poulter | Paperback & ePub

Despite our best intentions, many of us struggle to consistently reflect Jesus in our leadership. The Gospels suggest a new posture. Building on Jesus's intimacy with the Father, *Learning to Lead at the Feet of Jesus* highlights the rich relational setting in which Jesus exercised leadership and developed his followers into leaders. In the context of his intentional "withness," Jesus generously shared his life and authority with the Twelve.

Home Grown Leaders
Edgar J. Elliston | Paperback

Now a classic, *Home Grown Leaders* gives an approach for developing Christian leaders whether they be small group leaders, supervisors of multiple small groups, or pastors. It relies on both a biblical foundation and leadership theory. This book has been used to inform leadership trainers in many different parts of the world.

Developing Indigenous Leaders (SEANET 10)
Paul H. De Neui | Paperback & ePub

Leadership development remains the critical issue for mission endeavors around the world. How are leaders developed from the local context for the local context? What is the role of the expatriate in this process? The ten authors in this volume come from a wide range of ecclesial and national backgrounds and represent service in ten different Buddhist contexts of Asia. There is perhaps no more crucial issue than the development of dedicated indigenous leaders who will remain long after missionaries have returned home.

Available at missionbooks.com

www.ingramcontent.com/pod-product-compliance
Lightning Source LLC
Chambersburg PA
CBHW071241070526
44583CB00017B/2273